10

*Presented on the
occasion of Datacrown's
Tenth Anniversary*

*R.G. Taylor,
President and Chief Executive Officer*

December 1982.

Entering the Computer Age

The Computer Industry in Canada:
The First Thirty Years

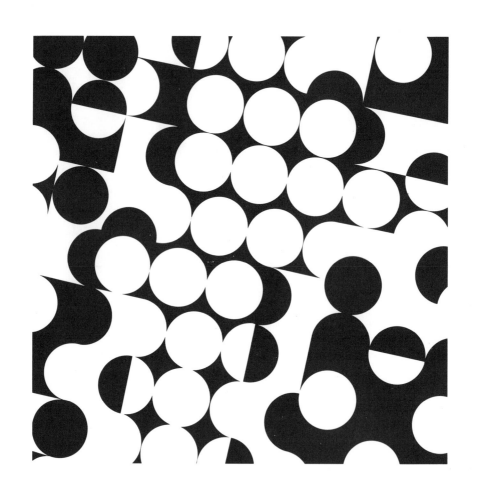

Entering
the Computer
Age

The Computer Industry in Canada:
The First Thirty Years

BEVERLEY J. BLEACKLEY

JEAN LaPRAIRIE

Published in association with

DATACROWN INC.

by

The Book Society of Canada Limited
Agincourt   Canada

Canadian Cataloguing in Publication Data
Bleackley, Beverley J.
  Entering the computer age

Includes index.
ISBN 0-7725-0015-0

1. Computer industry – Canada – History. I. La
Prairie, Jean. II. Title.

HD9696.C63C32   338.4′762138195′0971   C82-095230-3

Design/Robert Garbutt Productions
Printed and bound in Canada by John Deyell Company

1 2 3 4 5 6 7 8 JD 88 87 86 85 84 83 82

Photo Credits

Permission to reproduce photographs is gratefully acknowledged as follows. Page
numbers on which illustrations appear are listed after each source.
Leonard Casciato 85; Confederation Life Insurance Company 90; Datacrown Inc. 94;
Dr. Kelly Gotlieb 86, 88; Honeywell Ltd. *(courtesy of Patrick Suddick)* 92, 93; I.B.M.
Canada Ltd. 91; The Manufacturers Life Insurance Company 87; I.P. Sharp Associates
89; TranSyt Canada Inc. *(courtesy of Lyman Richardson)* 91

Authors' Note

Many people in the computer and data communications industries gave generously of their time, and freely opened their memory banks, to make this book possible. Our thanks to all. Because of time and space limitations, we have had to be somewhat selective in our discussions of each industry segment. We apologize in advance to any who may have been inadvertently omitted. We have tried to be up-to-date at time of writing, but as with any industry, changes will continually occur. The final chapter of any history remains always to be written.

B. J. BLEACKLEY
J. LaPRAIRIE

Contents

PART THREE
The Seventies and Beyond

Preface

THIS BOOK CHRONICLES the development of the computer industry in Canada—an industry which offers Canadians the prospect of a more productive and prosperous society, if we apply wisely what we have learned about the use and management of information in the creation of goods and services.

When our company, Datacrown Inc., began to consider ways in which we might observe our 10th anniversary in 1982, the idea of sponsoring a book on the history of the computer industry appealed very strongly to us. We felt that such a book would contribute to a better understanding and appreciation of this important industry, of which we are proud to be a part. It should also, we felt, provide an immensely interesting account of how a fairly small number of dedicated and resourceful individuals created the early infrastructure of data processing in Canada, and then, joined by others, pushed ahead with advances in hardware, innovative programs, and new ways of delivering computing services. The result, of course, is a society in which, by the 1980s, the computer has become all-pervasive.

We are very pleased that two of Canada's most able writers on computer subjects, Beverley Bleackley and Jean LaPrairie, agreed to undertake the writing of this book. We asked only that they produce a book which would be balanced in its treatment of the various sectors of the industry, and which would fairly recognize the contributions of those companies and individuals who have played a significant role in computing since we first entered on the computer age in the early 1950s. We think they have met these goals admirably. The result is an account that will be of interest to anyone with a desire to understand how Canada's computer industry came into being, and how it has developed in response to the opportunities of the past three decades.

The future of the computer industry in Canada will be tied closely to the general economic decisions that will be made in the coming decade, and to the attitudes that we Canadians develop as we move into an era in which the creation and use of information becomes one of our most important economic activities. By better understanding how we've arrived where we are, we will be better equipped to chart our course into the future.

R.G. TAYLOR
President and Chief Executive Officer
Datacrown Inc.
December, 1982

Entering the Computer Age

The Computer Industry in Canada:
The First Thirty Years

The state
of the industry today

"**D**ATA COMMUNICATIONS, COMPUTER services, and software. These are the strengths of the Canadian computer industry. The future lies in their development, exploitation and exportation."

Although the above words have not been credited to any one person within the computer industry, they have been voiced many times by various consultants, company presidents and industry watchers over the past few years. They have also been heeded by a large number of small Canadian companies and by the vast majority of international and multinational foreign-owned computer manufacturers in this country.

Recent estimates by both foreign- and Canadian-owned companies in the computer industry indicate that they are exporting from Canada approximately 75 percent of their production quotas—to the United States, Europe, the Middle East, the Far East, South America—wherever there is a market for their equipment, software or expertise. That compares to a 50 percent average for companies operating out of the United States, according to figures printed in Datamation magazine. And it is good news to hear as well that Canadian companies are venturing abroad to create their own markets rather than waiting for the world to beat a path to their doors.

Canadians have every reason to be proud of the contribution the computer/communications industry is making to the international scene. Across the world, Canada is recognized as a leader in communications and networking capability, with the hardware and software to back up the claim. Many Canadian users have led the way in the application of communications to their day-to-day operations. Canadian coast-to-coast online interactive banking networks have been imitated in the United States and abroad, often through cooperation with Canadian banks. A number of Canadian high technology firms including Spar Aerospace, SED Systems, Telesat Canada and others have contributed to the U.S. space program and have been publicly recognized for their contributions. The Canadian developed Telidon has been accepted as one of the three videotex systems classified as world standards. Telecommunications products, word processing equipment and video display terminals manufactured in Canada are successfully marketed in other countries.

The newest buzzword in data communications is "local area networking," a generic term used to describe the capability of connecting various pieces of office equipment (computers, video display terminals, word processors, facsimile machines, dictation and transcription equipment, photocopiers, etc.) together by cables and modems or data sets to allow information to be shared within an office or building. The Canadian companies operating in this area are too numerous to mention individually, although a great deal of significant research and development is now underway in this country. Particular emphasis has been placed on data switching, the integration of voice and data and the application of fibre optics to networking.

Software expertise from Canadian firms and branches of multinational companies is recognized around the world. As an example, Honeywell Information Systems of Toronto was awarded the worldwide mandate within the Honeywell organization for the development of computer-assisted learning software to be used on the company's computer equipment. Other smaller firms are creating software which has been adopted by large multinationals for use on their equipment across the world.

Many computing services firms, including Canada Systems Group, Comtech, Datacrown, Real Time Datapro, I.P. Sharp and Systemhouse have established themselves as world-class software and timesharing organizations.

Operating in an international market creates a series of universal social and political issues that might not be as noticeable in a strictly domestic arena. Import and export tariffs and duties on equipment, supplies and services are matters of concern to users and suppliers. Transborder data flow gives rise to the question of where data should be processed and whether jobs may be lost if the processing is done in another country. This also raises the problems of security and privacy of information relating both to individuals and companies. Canadians have had to come to terms with their own ideas on these subjects. As yet, there still seems to be a long way to go before these problems are resolved.

The groundwork for the software and communications capabilities for which Canada has become famous was laid in the 1950s. The early work done in such organizations as Computing Devices, Ferranti Electric, the University of Toronto, Trans Canada Airlines, the National Research Council, Atomic Energy of Canada Limited, as well as the multinational computer firms of IBM and Univac helped pave the way for future technological innovation and entrepreneurial activities.

Although the face of the industry has changed substantially over the past 30 years, the forces that drove it in the beginning are still in effect today. The geographical distances and diversities created a demand for communications capabilities to transmit data over telephone lines rather than by physical means. The size of Canadian user firms (in relation to their counterparts in the U.S.) meant that computers had to be used for multiple applications rather than being dedicated to one purpose, and this led to the need for more software.

Canadians have met these challenges boldly and imaginatively. Their achievements, past and present, suggest a bright future for Canada in the computer age.

PART ONE

The Fifties

How It All Began

*F*ROM THE BEGINNING of what was to be known as the Information Age, Canadians were quick to recognize the potential of the new electronic technology. At first, only a handful were caught up to the excitement of exploiting this technology. However, the small band of pioneers would increase, and their achievements would dramatically impact Canada's future.

1

The people who got things going

*T*ORONTO, MAY 18, 1949—"Huge pushbutton brain to be built at U of T" announced a headline in the Toronto *Globe and Mail*.

The "pushbutton brain" was UTEC (University of Toronto Electronic Computer), now recognized as one of Canada's early and remarkable achievements in computer technology. The story behind the headline had actually begun two years earlier. In 1947 three University of Toronto professors—B.A. Griffith, V.G. Smith, and A.F.C. Stevenson—received a grant from the National Research Council and the Defence Research Board to investigate digital computers and eventually to design and build a machine.

A year later the group hired Calvin C. (Kelly) Gotlieb to oversee the project. Toronto-born Gotlieb was a recent Ph.D. graduate in physics and a member of the U of T faculty. In the years ahead he was to earn an international reputation for his teaching, publications and work with computer groups throughout the world. In 1948 he was 27 years old and looked even younger.

"Kelly Gotlieb was thin, he had a thick shock of dark hair, he wore glasses, and often a bow tie," one of his former students recalls. "The first time I saw him walk into a classroom, I thought he was an undergraduate."

Looking back on the initiation of the UTEC project, Dr. Gotlieb says, "From the beginning, we had two goals. The first was to do some computations for Atomic Energy of Canada Limited

(AECL), which had no computing facilities at its Chalk River laboratories. The second was to acquire some computing capabilities at the University."

To meet the first goal, the group assembled some punched card equipment, including an IBM 602A calculator. A team was organized to do the necessary calculations for Chalk River and the Defence Research Board.

A second team, composed mostly of graduate students, was hired to explore the engineering possibilities of building an electronic computer at the University. This design team was headed by Josef Kates and Alfred Ratz.

Originally, Dr. Gotlieb believed that the fastest way to acquire computing facilities would be to build a copy of the Bell Model 6 Relay Computer that had been produced at the Bell Telephone Laboratories in New Jersey. He visited the Laboratories, where he was given "about two cubic yards" of blueprints for the Model 6. Crossing the border with this bulky burden on his return to Canada, he encountered what may have been the first problem in transborder data flow.

The documents were marked "Restricted", and Dr. Gotlieb refused to let the customs official examine them. A somewhat heated discussion followed. Eventually, the official decided to follow the customs regulations that applied to bringing in blueprints for a factory. He put the documents on a scale and charged duty according to their weight.

The copy of the Bell Relay Computer was never built. "Bell required a $20,000 licensing fee," Dr. Gotlieb explains. "Whether it was the fee or whether NRC had decided the future lay in electronic rather than in relay machines, I do not know. However, I think now it was the right decision."

As the development of UTEC progressed, a number of U of T graduate students and faculty members worked on various aspects of the project. An early member of the electronic design team was James Richardson, who left about 1949 to become chief designer at the Los Alamos National Laboratory in New Mexico. Len Casciato took Richardson's place and worked at the Computation Centre until the early fifties. R.F. (Bob) Johnson entered the scene as the designer of the UTEC bulk storage system. Working with Ratz on circuit design was Harold Stein.

University of Toronto professor Pat Hume wrote one of the first programs for UTEC. Harvey Gellman, who was working on his Ph.D. in Mathematics, was also an active member of the group.

The acknowledged "leading light" of the electronic design team was Joe Kates. Born in Vienna in 1921, he was one of the refugees who fled to England when Germany invaded Austria in 1938. To his university colleagues he appeared brilliant, confident, energetic, persuasive and "a steamroller in conversation."

"We were a very young, brash and green group," Dr. Gotlieb says. "But things were wide open, information was freely exchanged, and members of even such an unlikely group as ours were made welcome at such prestigious institutions as the Princeton University Institute for Advanced Studies.

"Throughout the years when the prototype UTEC was being evolved, all of us at the Computation Centre shared a sense of high excitement," Dr. Gotlieb continues. "We had a feeling that we had a tiger by the tail. There was a real awareness that something new and important was going on."

In 1951, the prototype electronic computer was completed. The machine is described in a paper presented by Bob Johnson at the Association for Computing Machinery meeting, jointly sponsored by ACM and the U of T in 1952. The meeting was the first computer conference to be held in Canada. Mr. Johnson's paper in the Proceedings describes UTEC as: "a parallel binary digital machine, using a one-address code, 12-binary-digit words, 8 orders, and a 512-word Williams electrostatic store. Internal orders are carried out in 120 microseconds. Terminal output includes punched paper tape input, tape and typewriter output. A magnetic tape auxiliary store is to be added in the near future."

UTEC was housed in a former lecture room on the U of T campus. With almost 1,000 vacuum and 12 cathode ray tubes, the system required a great deal of power and generated an enormous amount of heat. In operation, it was a dramatic sight, with the pattern of the entire memory visible as red, green and blue lights flashed across the tubes.

"Because of the very primitive instruction code—we had no high level languages or anything like that—programming UTEC was very laborious," Dr. Kates says. "However, we wrote a number of sub-routines. We programmed the machine for multiplication and division capabilities, as well as for other arithmetic functions.

"We also programmed it for playing games—making it perhaps one of the first computers to be used for that purpose."

Reliability was extremely low, primarily because of the cathode ray tube storage system, which was highly sensitive to power disturbances. The U of T group was happy if the computer worked an hour without a failure, and often there were only minutes between failures.

"UTEC was basically an experimental design intended to advance the state of the art and to be used for research purposes," Dr. Kates says. "However, we hoped the university would eventually develop full-scale computers for major applications."

This was not to be. Due to a strange interrelationship of the events which followed, work on the prototype geared down and eventually came to a halt. In 1951, there was an unexpected change in the British government. The supposedly well-entrenched Labour Party was ousted by the Conservatives. Immediately the new government cancelled all outstanding purchase orders exceeding £100,000. Among these orders was a Ferranti Mark 1 computer, made by the British company and almost ready for delivery to the United Kingdom Atomic Energy Authority.

In Canada, the National Research Council and the Defence Research Board, who had sponsored and financed the U of T computer development group, urged them to buy the unexpectedly available Ferranti machine. The sponsors wanted computing power, and they wanted it immediately. The pressure—and an additional incentive of increased funding for research—were too strong to resist. Eventually, with reluctance, the university agreed to acquire the new computer.

"Those of us who'd worked on developing UTEC were tremendously disappointed," says Len Casciato. "We were thoroughly familiar with the work that was going on elsewhere in the world, and we knew UTEC was equal to the best, putting us in the front line of development of high speed storage digital computers. We'd felt that we just couldn't miss."

Was the failure to produce a full-scale computer based on UTEC an opportunity lost for Canada? After 30 years, this continues to be a moot question. Some of those involved in the project still believe that the decision to acquire the Ferranti was a crippling blow to proven Canadian leadership in the new electronics field. Others argue that embarking on the production of a full-scale machine would have been disastrous, given the magnitude of development costs and the limitation of university resources. At any rate, when Len Casciato visited the University of Toronto in the mid-fifties, he found UTEC completely dismantled, with parts of the machine being sold for scrap.

Ferut comes to Canada

In April, 1952, the Ferranti computer was delivered. Dr. Beatrice Worsley of the Computation Centre named it Ferut (FERranti — University of Toronto). According to Dr. Gotlieb, Ferut was the first electronic computer to be purchased in Canada.

"Immediately we were plunged into the excitement of having a very early computer and of solving the problems of using it," he says.

Certainly there were problems. The Computation Centre staff had to learn how to handle systematically large inputs and outputs. The machine was highly error prone, and they had to check data, check programs and check the computer.

Their first project using Ferut was the computation of water levels for the St. Lawrence Seaway. At the time, negotiations were underway between Ontario Hydro and New York State as to the location of the Seaway, and whether it would be an all-Canadian or a joint Canada-U.S. venture. Hydro, with the aid of Ferut and a U of T software team headed by Dr. Gotlieb, did massive calculations, including three alternate routes for the Seaway. The impressive evidence they produced played an important role in the final decision as to the Seaway's location.

"This is a good example, and an early one, of the political influence of computer calculations," Dr. Gotlieb says.

Ferut was also used in an early data communications project. The University of Toronto provided computing services to a number of other universities without cost. In the early fifties, researchers at the University of Saskatchewan in Saskatoon sent data to Toronto for computation on Ferut. Ferut used five-level paper tape input, the same as the paper tape used by teleprinters. To prepare their data, the U of S researchers borrowed a teleprinter paper punch from Canadian National Telegraphs, adapting the punch by pasting adhesive tape marked with Ferut binary code on the keys. At first, the tapes were sent back and forth between the two universities by mail.

In 1955, however, CN was approached about the possibility of using a teleprinter circuit for a direct communication link. CN agreed to provide the circuits during off-time evening hours and loaned additional teleprinter machines to the U of S. Local telephone loops linking the university with the telegraph office were established. Direct transmission of data began on December 15.

The program tapes were sent from Saskatoon like any other message through the telegraph circuit and line equipment. In Toronto, Ferut performed the computations, punched the results on paper tape and sent the data back to Saskatoon, where hard copy was produced on a page printer.

Coordinating the operation in Saskatoon was J.H. (Harry) Toop, now affiliated with the University of Windsor's Department of Mathematics and president of his own company. He was a student of the U of S, working night shifts as a CN telegraph operator.

Weekly telecomputing continued for almost a year, until the University of Saskatchewan acquired its own computer, an LGP-30. The quick turnaround time for computations made a significant contribution to the research projects underway at the University of Saskatchewan.

Ferut provided computing services at the University of Toronto until 1958. Despite the unreliability of the machine, the Computation Centre did an enormous amount of calculations for other universities, business and government organizations. In 1954, the first Canadian-designed compiler was produced by Beatrice Worsley and Pat Hume.

For a number of years, the Centre was the instrument for AECL computing, with Dr. Harvey Gellman eventually becoming the person responsible for Chalk River work. Later, as an AECL employee, he set up the electronic computer section at Chalk River. "I was stationed in Toronto, using the Ferranti computer, and visited Chalk River a couple of times a month to keep in touch with the scientists and engineers," says Gellman. When he left to become a private consultant, forming H.S. Gellman & Company, AECL became one of his clients and has remained a client throughout the years.

However, by the mid-fifties, the Computation Centre realized it needed a successor to the Ferranti machine. In 1958 Ferut was replaced by an IBM 650.

"We had lived with our Ferranti machine in splendid isolation for quite a long time, because Ferranti changed the instruction code of the machine right after delivering ours," says Dr. Gotlieb. "So we had been, roughly speaking, programming only for ourselves. The 650 was really a step down in computing capacity, but brought us into contact with the IBM world."

Canada's first computer manufacturer

During the fifties, the University was not the only Canadian centre of computer-oriented activities.

At Ferranti Electric Limited (later Ferranti-Packard) in Toronto, a team of engineers pioneered the design and production of world-class technology computers. Director of research until 1955 was Dr. Arthur Porter, who had come to Ferranti from England, where the parent company was headquartered. When he left the Canadian group to enter academic life, first in England and later in Canada, he was succeeded by storage specialist, Kenyon Taylor. Logic design architect was Fred Longstaff, now vice president, systems and software development, of ESE Limited, Toronto. Mr. Longstaff had become "hooked on computing" while a student at the University of Toronto. In exchange for computer time, he'd written programs for Ferut.

Other members of the early Ferranti group included Gordon Lang, who was primarily responsible for communications in the systems, chief engineer Tom Cranston and engineer Les Wood, who later became chief engineer and has remained with Ferranti.

It was a brilliant team, and the computers they built were

years ahead of similar developments in other countries. Dr. Porter calls it "the most incredible group of people I have ever worked with." Other members of the group speak with equal respect, almost awe, of their colleagues. Fred Longstaff, for example, is described by his former colleagues as "a tremendously modest guy, who is without doubt one of the brightest people in Canada—a logic designer, engineer and programmer par excellence." Kenyon Taylor is referred to by his one-time associates as "an unsung genius." Among other accomplishments, Taylor anticipated the development of xerography.

This was the group who, in the late fifties, put together a naval data acquisition and target tracking system that included the first computer network in which three physically separate digital processing systems were interconnected through radio channels and operated as a single system. Today such networks are common. Twenty-five years ago they represented a significant break-through in technical achievement.

"The system, called Datar, demonstrated what electronics might be able to do for the Navy some day in operations such as tracking targets," Mr. Longstaff says. It included electronic equipment at a shore station and on two mine sweepers operating on Lake Ontario.

Since this was before the days of transistors, the system included some 30,000 vacuum tubes. "We fitted out the mine sweepers with tons of electronics and diesel generators and air conditioners to cool the lot. It's a wonder we didn't turn them over in the lake," Mr. Longstaff comments.

The mean time between system failures was 15 to 20 minutes. However, the maintenance crew was so skillful that the mean time for making repairs was generally about 30 seconds.

Datar provoked considerable interest, and Ferranti prepared presentations and introductory lectures for visitors. "What the visitors didn't know," Mr. Longstaff says, "was that at the back of the lecture room there were a red light and a green light. When the red light was on, you knew the system was down and you kept on talking. If the green light went on, you stopped talking and rushed the visitors down the hall to the demonstration area as fast as possible."

Shortly afterward, about 1955, Ferranti developed the first semi-conductor computer using printed circuits and designed on a modular basis. It was delivered to the Canadian Post Office for sorting mail—some three years ahead of similar developments in other countries.

Ferranti—and a number of people who had been involved with the University of Toronto Computation Centre—also contributed to the development of Canada's first airline seat reservation system. According to Lyman Richardson, who was the TransCanada Airlines (TCA—now Air Canada) person in charge of the project, the TCA computer was the first transistorized computer built and used in commercial service. "To take a scientific computer and put a general purpose inventory program on it was a real breakthrough," he says.

Mr. Richardson began working on the project in 1953, preparing a report on the reservations and communications requirements for the airline. When TCA approved the report, Adalia Ltd., a Montreal-based company headed by radar pioneer Sir Robert Watson-Watt, was awarded the contract to produce the conceptual design. Adalia had engaged Joe Kates and Len Casciato to do the design work, which involved demonstrations on the U of T Ferut.

TransCanada then negotiated with Ferranti to supply the terminals and communications devices to interface with Ferut. "To test the system's mobility, we put the terminals in cars and moved them around the city, giving demonstrations at different locations," Mr. Richardson says. "When the system was eventually demonstrated to the airline's board of directors, it took them less than five minutes to give the go-ahead to the project."

Ferranti was awarded the contract to supply some 400 terminals, and later, after tendering, a contract to build the central computer facilities, two members of Harvey Gellman's company, Mike Lucas and Dennis Wray, wrote the software.

"We all worked together as a team," Mr. Richardson says. "Because of the cost of systems in those days, we had to engineer every binary digit. Just one digit was an enormous consideration. We also had to design our messages for the shortest length and the fastest time. We had to design the communications network—and that was the first time a transaction-oriented network had ever been run."

The central processing unit built for the reservations system (called ReserVec I) was the Ferranti Gemini. As its name implies, it was a parallel computer system. Each of the two main components was a general purpose computer. Mass storage, in the form of drums and tapes, was shared, as were output devices. As each reservation request came in, one or the other computer would deal with it. According to Mr. Longstaff, "The two of them together gave you approximately twice the capacity of one. And if one failed, you could continue to run with half the usual capacity." Input was with cards, designed by Mr. Richardson, on which requests were made by pencil marks.

ReserVec I became an integral part of TransCanada Airline's operations. "It could measure supply and demand and give us loading on flights far in advance," Lyman Richardson says. "It produced flight arrival/departure information, as well as its own statistics."

He adds that in the 10 years that the system operated before being upgraded, its average downtime per year was only 120 seconds. On its busiest day, it handled a quarter of a million transactions.

The computers developed at Ferranti proved that a Canadian group could put together computer systems second to none. But few, if any further steps were taken to capitalize on Canada's early strengths in computer leadership.

2

The multinationals shape up in Canada

THE LARGE MULTINATIONAL computer corporations, all foreign owned and most with corporate headquarters in the United States, did not just happen upon the Canadian scene with the advent of data processing.

Prior to 1950, virtually all were doing business in Canada and had offices in this country. The one exception: Control Data Canada, did not set up operations in Canada until the early sixties, although its early computers were distributed here by Computing Devices of Canada in the late fifties.

International Business Machines had a booming office equipment business with typewriters, time clocks and unit record equipment. Burroughs Business Machines Ltd. dealt mainly with accounting equipment. Univac, now Sperry Inc. and then known as Remington-Rand, was in the typewriter and office equipment business and became the first multinational company in the computer business in Canada. NCR, as National Cash Register Company, sold MICR (Magnetic Ink Character Recognition), cheque clearing and posting systems as well as its cash registers, mostly to the retail and banking establishments. Honeywell Ltd.'s main business had been in thermostats, temperature regulators and controls.

Although these were to be the feature players in the drama about to unfold, there were the extras and bit players also waiting in the wings. Xerox had a hold on the xerographic and photocopy market, and Canadian General Electric Company was involved in microwave and multiplex equipment.

Aside from the work done at Ferranti Electric Limited, the major pieces of hardware were manufactured in the United States until the beginning of the sixties, when some complete systems were manufactured here. International Business Machines (IBM) and Remington-Rand (Univac) led the way for the first half of the decade and were joined at the end of the fifties by Burroughs, Honeywell, NCR, Xerox, RCA and Canadian General Electric.

Although Univac had been the first computer on the market, in Canada IBM quickly gained the lead position and maintained it, even to the present.

"IBM's base of punched card and time clock users gave the company the insight and knowledge of their users' businesses and needs," says B.B. (Ike) Goodfellow, one of the first group of applied science representatives hired by IBM and now IBM's Ottawa branch manager. "It was really punched card accounting that gave birth to the commercial computing industry. Punched card spelled the end of bookkeeping equipment and the time clock era."

The first systems engineer in IBM Canada was John Aitchison, who started with the company in 1951. Mr. Aitchison was a man of impressive appearance, balding, tall, with a learned, scientific look about him. He added credibility to what IBM did, and had "charisma in a big way," says a former colleague. During the sixties, Mr. Aitchison would be called to the United States to become IBM U.S. systems engineering manager, and later director of the IBM Systems Research Institute. He would return to Canada in 1976 to head up Bell-Northern Software Research Inc. Unfortunately, John Aitchison passed away as research material was being gathered for this book. He will be remembered by the people in the computer industry as a capable manager with technical integrity and the ability to identify with the technical community.

Three young salesmen hired that same year were Bill Moore (who would become president of IBM Canada, then later president of Consolidated Computer Inc. before forming Network Data Systems), George Kerwin (who became Hamilton branch manager for IBM Canada and today is manager of marketing with Canada Systems Group) and Carl Corcoran (who worked his way up through the ranks of IBM to his present position of vice-president, operations).

"When I joined IBM in 1951, we had 90 per cent of the punched card and unit record business and the other 10 per cent was all Remington-Rand," recalls Bill Moore. "There weren't any computers as such in IBM then. In fact, I didn't hear of a computer until 1953 when suddenly IBM's customers said that we had better come up with computers or lose their business. At first, the salesman installed his own machines and wired the boards and held the customer's hand, and did it all with the help of junior salesmen if necessary. Gradually, the systems engineer became the man the customer counted on more and more, because he was the person who could come in and fix the programs."

Mr. Aitchison was given the task of setting up a force of applied science representatives—later called systems engineers—knowledgeable in the installation of the new IBM computers which would soon be brought up from the United States. This force would also be required to assist customers in the operation of their computers. The first recruits were young, eager recent university graduates like Walter Smuk, George Richardson, Wesley Graham, Ike Goodfellow, Elmer Talvila, Conrad Maheux and Ingo Grossman.

Raw recruits all, with only a smattering of knowledge about these new-fangled machines, the applied science representatives and the salesmen learned about computers, at times just one step ahead of the users.

"Often we had no education or training in the systems we were asked to install," says Wes Graham, now a computer science professor and director of the Computer Systems Group at the University of Waterloo. "John Aitchison would hand us the manual the night before, then introduce us to the clients the following day as 'our expert on this machine.' We flew by the seat of our pants, but we had to make those systems work. It was all nerve."

Ike Goodfellow credits many of the early users as the driving force behind the industry. "There were a number of leading-edge users during the fifties in particular," he says. "They were pioneer people who recognized the potential of computers, sometimes in areas that we hadn't even thought of. But they knew their own requirements and were willing to experiment and take a chance on applying computing power to their applications."

Companies such as Orenda Engines, the company that developed engines for the A. V. Roe (AVRO) Aircraft Company, Ontario Hydro and Steel Company of Canada (Stelco) were pioneers on a machine called the IBM Card Programmable Calculator (CPC) in 1951.

"The CPC was really a 'lash-up' of a number of different machines—a card reader, a processor, a storage device and a printer," says Mr. Goodfellow. "The card went in one end, data was read off the card and flowed through the machines and their connecting wires to be printed out at the other end. It wasn't really a computer, but it was the closest thing we had to one at the time. It was the company's first attempt at using programming languages with punched cards. Although a number of CPCs were installed here by major companies, they were used mostly for mathematical computations."

These early machines were still too cumbersome to be used widely for business applications. They were generally kept in the back room, with strictly controlled environmental conditions, and were the domain of the scientist, the mathematician and the professional data processor or programmer. The machines and the people who worked with them used an arcane language all their own, which made it difficult for non-computer types to understand what was going on.

However, by 1953, another advance in technology changed and improved the configurations of computers and made them more acceptable for business. Magnetic storage in the form of magnetic drums, disks and cores created faster and cheaper storage and memory devices, replacing the slow and not always reliable punched cards.

The equipment was still not as user friendly as later models would be, but it was a step in the right direction.

Computers become commercial

IBM introduced the 650, its first drum storage machine in 1956. Remington-Rand came on the market at the same time with the

Univac 2. Competition between these two suppliers and their users became fierce. It was a toss-up to see which users would be the first to install the new models, whose applications would be the most advanced. The life insurance companies became leaders in the application of computer technology.

According to Jasper Moore, then vice president of Crown Life Insurance Company (he retired from the company in 1976), the life insurance companies had been working on automating their policy files since the end of World War II. Throughout the 1950s, companies like Crown Life had been looking for a method to consolidate the myriad files necessary to the life insurance industry. They had gone to punched cards and tabulators in an attempt to move closer to consolidation, but most did not arrive at an acceptable solution until the early 1960s.

"We had separate files for each different piece of information on a policy holder," Mr. Moore says, "as well as files for each individual policy a holder had taken out. The amount of information was staggering. And the errors we later found when we automated were embarrassing. We were constantly looking for ways of bringing all the information together into a common data base to improve our effectiveness and save time searching through policy holder information.

"A great help to users was the Tape Users Conference, an unorganized group of people who were interested in the aspects and applications of computer tape," he continues. "That group was the forerunner of today's Canadian Information Processing Society. It included people from Crown Life, Confederation Life, Manufacturers Life, IDA (Independent Druggists Association), General Motors, Air Canada, Imperial Oil and Stelco, among others. We got together to discuss similar problems and their solutions, and how computer technology could apply. We were all new to the game."

Crown Life itself did not actually install a computer system until 1961, although the company did use unit record, card and tabulating equipment until that time. "We at Crown Life ordered every IBM machine as soon as it was announced, including a 650 and a 705," says Mr. Moore. "But we didn't get around to installing one, until we got a 7070 in 1961. We would study their capabilities in relation to our application and realize that they just wouldn't do all we wanted to do at that time."

Other life insurance companies were more adventurous.

Manufacturers Life Insurance Company was the first Canadian firm to install an IBM 650.

"When we installed the 650 at Manufacturers Life in March 1956 that company became the first commercial user of an IBM machine in Canada," recalls Ike Goodfellow. "Later that year, another 650 was brought in to be part of the IBM exhibit at the Canadian National Exhibition (CNE) in Toronto. At that time, the CNE was the only large exhibition held. There were no such things as computer shows, automotive shows, etc. The CNE was the place to show every new piece of household equipment, furniture, all the new car models, farm equipment and new technology. We exhibited the 650 not as a computer, but as an 'electronic brain.'"

The second installation of a 650 in Canada was at KCS Data Control in Toronto.

Soon after, a 650 was installed at the IBM datacentre at 36 King Street East, in the Toronto downtown office. Walter Smuk remembers doing some programming on that computer for Hudson Stowe at Manufacturers Life during his first year with IBM.

"I had just taken the 650 course and considered myself still a novice with the company and on this particular machine," he recalls. "I had been working on a few assignments for John Aitchison when he suddenly pulled me off everything and told me to write some programs right away for Hudson Stowe. All other 'priorities' took second place when Manufacturers Life called. The actuarial work I did for them was the first program I wrote.

"We usually did the programming work right on the customer's premises," continues Walter Smuk. "But we did some work at the datacentre on the 650 under the guidance of Elmer Talvila who managed the datacentre at that time. I remember one of the applications we set up to demonstrate a parts explosion system for Massey Ferguson, and Bill Moore was the salesman. That demonstration sold them a 650."

Another early user of the 650 was Canadian National Railways (CNR). Arthur Mackey, who later went on to work for Univac, then struck out on his own with WM Electronics and Mohawk Data Systems, was in charge of the computer installation at CNR.

"We used it mainly for the payroll application," says Mr. Mackey. "There were 117,000 CNR employees across the country and we decided to centralize the payroll, which had previously been done in each separate location. I recall when Donald Gordon, who was the president of CNR then, had his private car hooked onto a train going to Prince Rupert. When the train stopped at a small station along the way, and didn't move, he sent someone to find out what was the matter. The crew refused to go any farther because their pay cheques weren't there as they should have been. The hazards of centralization were that we had to process the cheques in Montreal on the computer, then fly them to the west coast—and to every other location across Canada—for distribution. Sometimes they were late."

"That payroll application caused us some headaches," he continues, "but it also once showed me how people in the industry in those days really did help each other out. The first time we processed the payroll centrally, we worked on it for three days solid without very much sleep. It had to be ready by noon of the fourth day so the employees could cash their cheques before the bank closed, and we realized that we might not make it. The union was very tough in the railway and had called the newspapers saying we were going to be late because of this new computer system. To get over the hurdles, I contacted a manager I knew at Eaton's and they set up a counter right in the store in Toronto to cash the cheques.

"I guess we were all in the same boat in those days. Computers were new, we were a smaller user community, we all knew each other. There wasn't the competition between users that there is today. There was more togetherness."

The railway had also set up a tracing system to keep track of the location of their trains across the country. Although it was successfully computerized, Art Mackey says that some of the employees were skeptical.

"I went to Winnipeg to check on the operations," he says, "and walked into a room where there were about 35 people sitting there still filling in the books by hand. They knew we had an automatic system, but figured that the 'other' system, the computer, would probably break down eventually. And they wanted to have complete and accurate manual records just in case."

Snow White and the Seven Dwarfs

While IBM was having a great success with the 650, the competition from Univac was heating up. At the end of 1956 and into early 1957, IBM lost its accounts at London Life, Sun Life and Ontario Hydro to Univac 2 installations. The effect of these installations on IBM was, according to those who were there at the time, devastating. They didn't understand how such long-standing customers could leave the fold. What had they done wrong?

They really hadn't done anything wrong. The competition was just becoming more intense and the users were seeing some alternatives coming on the market.

It was at this time in history that Honeywell, Burroughs, NCR, RCA, Canadian General Electric and Xerox were beginning to make their presence known. Now, instead of just two salesmen knocking on their doors, the users had anywhere up to eight lining up to see them.

All the companies were competing for competent salespeople and systems engineers. IBM still had the lion's share of the market and, therefore, attracted the most candidates.

People like Jake Avery, Bruce Campbell, Helmut Lerch, Ted White, Jack Kyle, Guy Renfer, Dick Taylor, Larry Shick, George Fierheller, Mers Kutt, Gerry Meinzer, Mike Howe, Gerry Wanless, Doug Marshall and others joined the ranks of IBM sales and systems employees. Harry Sheppard was on board as Canadian president. Joe King was national sales manager. Karl Moeser was the district manager, Bill Moore became Toronto downtown branch manager and Bernie Kuehn was then manager of the London branch.

The dynasty that was to shape IBM's Canadian organization for the next 25 years had its beginnings during this period. The team of Harry Sheppard and Joe King helped to create an atmosphere that fostered entrepreneurship among IBM employees. Mr. Sheppard began the Canadianization of the company, carried on by his successors. King was respected throughout the industry. It was considered a great loss to the industry, as well as a personal tragedy, when he went down in the Trans Canada Airlines crash just outside Montreal in November, 1963.

IBM's downtown Toronto office was the key place to be in the 1950s in order to make it within that company, according to the early players.

"Karl Moeser had a very definite attitude about what you had to do to survive in IBM," says Richard G. Taylor, now president of Datacrown Inc. "His approach to staffing was straightforward: if it looked as if you were going to be successful in IBM, you were brought in to work in the downtown Toronto office. If there were some doubt, but also some possibility, you went to the Toronto uptown office. Other than that, you were banished to Ottawa. Even though IBM had offices across the country, those were the only three that existed in Karl's world. It all seems out of proportion now, specifically with the success of the Ottawa alumni in the industry today."

Mr. Moeser was also a stickler for proper dress, as was the whole of the IBM corporation, according to many early IBMers.

During one business meeting, it is said that one IBM sales representative posed the following question to Karl Moeser. "Mr. Moeser, you're sales manager here. Why are we so strict on dress code?" Mr. Moeser reportedly replied, "The successful businessman is wearing this type of clothing, and we must conform to his code of dress. When businessmen begin to wear bathing suits to work, we will too."

The image of the IBM salesman in a three-piece blue pinstriped suit persisted over the following decades as well. But there was more.

"Bill Moore called me into his office," recalls Mike Howe, "and said 'You don't wear a hat, do you?' When I said 'No, I don't,' he just said 'Get one.' I bought a hat and when I walked into the office, four different people stopped and laughed at me between the front door and my desk. But I wore that hat for years, until one day all of a sudden IBM people weren't wearing hats anymore. I think it changed when Jack Brent became president in 1963, because he didn't like wearing a hat. So, of course, the dress code changed."

In addition to his attitudes on behavior and dress, though, Karl Moeser is remembered as an extremely capable manager who stood out as an able businessman. "He made things happen," says

Ike Goodfellow. "Most of the people who came out of 36 King Street East have advanced to where they are because Karl Moeser and John Aitchison were capable managers."

At the same time, the other computer manufacturers were also known as much by the personalities who led their management teams as for their equipment.

At Honeywell, Patrick Suddick was organizing the computer division and making a start on hiring a sales and service staff. Gene Racicot and 'Rocky' Martino had established a competent systems centre at Univac, and Bill Wilbur was responsible for Univac sales. Bill Wade was starting to form a nucleus of systems people within the Burroughs organization. These people, and others, helped lay the foundation for the burgeoning industry that was to follow over the next decades.

"IBM was extremely big by the time the rest of us got into the market," explains Pat Suddick. "And Univac was beginning to slip somewhat. The media began calling the computer companies Snow White and the Seven Dwarfs. The rest of us, the dwarfs, were whittling away at 15 per cent of the business, which isn't much. However, we had faith that the business was going to grow if we could only stick with it.

"I started up Honeywell's computer division in 1958," he continues, "when the Avro Arrow fell. Honeywell wondered what they would do with me now that the Avro project was over, because they wanted to keep me on staff but didn't have a job for me. Someone suggested I go home and paint my house, but that didn't appeal to me. So I said 'How about my getting involved in the computer business?' They said 'What's that?' I had heard about it down in the United States and went down and got some more information and received permission to go ahead. I went on a course, supposed to be a 13-week course at Datamatic in Boston on computers. I was four days into the course when I got an urgent call to return to Canada to see a customer who was putting out a tender for a replacement computer. I never did get back to the training course. That was 1958. By the middle of 1959, I had built up a staff of about six or seven people to cover the whole country.

"It was close to five years before we even sold a computer,"

Mr. Suddick says in his characteristic jovial and down-to-earth way. "But we were in there plugging away. We 'dwarfs' developed a kind of rapport amongst ourselves. It was 'us' against the giant. And we were in there all the time, trying to chip away at the foundation."

The concentration of large computer systems was in the Toronto, Ottawa, Montreal triangle — the cities where the majority of head office sites were located. The oil company offices were mostly in Toronto. The insurance company head offices were either in Toronto or Montreal. The banks were divided between Toronto and Montreal. And the government was in Ottawa.

The "branch plant" economy of Canada had a telling effect on the computer industry. In general, the buying decision on a computer system was made in the United States (the majority of large organizations were U.S.-owned), and the Canadian subsidiary was obliged to go along with whatever had been chosen there. Sometimes the decision could be overturned, but it was very difficult.

"It was great if they had your system in the U.S. office," says Pat Suddick. "If they had someone else's, it was a difficult job to persuade them to consider yours. You had to have a good friend and good champion in the company that you were dealing with. We did get into some of those situations. Sometimes we won, sometimes we lost. But we never stopped trying."

Though the other suppliers had entered the market, the main competition until the end of the decade was still between IBM and Univac. IBM introduced the 705 system in 1957, facing the Univac 2 and Univac 3 along with Honeywell's Datamatic 800, Burroughs, B205, RCA's Bismac and NCR7's 390 series.

"We at IBM had been pretty devastated by the Univac sales to London Life, Sun Life and Ontario Hydro," says Ike Goodfellow. "We had to do something to bring ourselves out of the slump. The Confederation Life tender came up, and we were surprised to find that our main competitor on that one was RCA with their Bismac system. When we finally installed a 705 there, it was a great morale booster."

Another 705 was installed in Montreal in the Canadian Pacific Railway offices. "Eric Leslie at CPR was one of the real pioneer people who recognized the potential of computers," says Mr. Goodfellow. "At the time, there wasn't a railway in the world that was as advanced in data processing as CPR."

However, it was the 705 centre at Confederation Life that became the focal point for IBM in Canada. To offset some costs, Confederation rented back time to IBM. IBM used that installation as a second datacentre and a number of today's top industry figures got their start programming there.

At the same time, there was a Burroughs B205 installed at AECL in Chalk River, and another at Canadair in Montreal. Other users were beginning to look outside the IBM world. However IBM was still the main supplier.

"Statistics Canada, then the Dominion Bureau of Statistics, became a leading-edge user in the 1957 era," says Ike Goodfellow. "Rudy Zioto and Jack Marshall, the chief statistician, are recognized as pioneering users. Colin D'Ombraine at the Meteorological Bureau in Montreal was doing great things with computers then. So was Art Downing at A. V. Roe and the staff at Revenue Canada."

As the decade wore on, opportunities within the supplier side of the industry grew along with those on the user side. In addition to newcomers entering the field, there were a number of shifts or job changes among suppliers.

One of the major factors in the computer industry in 1959 was the application of the transistor and solid state technology to the computer. The transistor, 1/200th the size of the bulky vacuum tube, was being incorporated into televisions, radios, high fidelity systems and other electric and electronic pieces of equipment at a furious rate that year. Through its use, equipment was becoming smaller. It was only natural that the computer industry should adopt the technology as well.

IBM was the first on the market with their general purpose transistorized computer, the 1401 and the 1400 series. With the new technology, the computer also became smaller than its behemoth ancestors.

This opened the door for the other suppliers to create their own versions of these systems. It changed the complexion of the industry, since computer technology was now available to a wider range of users and applications.

Canadian suppliers and minor multinationals

While 'Snow White and the Seven Dwarfs' were battling it out in the large computer field, a number of smaller companies were quietly selling very small computer systems—the forerunners of today's microcomputers—across the country. The main markets were the scientific, electronic and research fields. The computers were often systems that were used for only one application, by a very small group of users within an organization. By connecting these systems to large mainframes, these companies had an early version of distributed data processing.

The suppliers—in particular Computing Devices of Canada (later Computing Devices Company), The McBee Company, Royal Precisions Ltd. and Leigh Instruments—were all located in the Montreal and Ottawa area. Some were subsidiaries of small American firms. Others were Canadian companies distributing U.S.-built systems along with their own electronic products.

Although not technically in the computer business at the beginning of the 1950s, Computing Devices has been a major Canadian firm contributing to the computer industry over the years. Founded in 1948 by Joseph Norton and George Glinski, Computing Devices got its start through a product that was developed at the National Research Council. The product, the Position and Homing Indicator (PHI), was a device for airplanes that could track a plane's flight movements and indicate the route back 'home' to the airbase. PHI was not considered a computer, but used the latest in computer technology for the time. From that came a device called the Moving Map Display which kept a map running in front of the airplane's pilot and navigator to show what ground was underneath and what had been covered. Both products were based on radar techniques and were the result of research on ways to improve navigational technology.

Technology for the military was the domain of the Defence Research Telecommunications Establishment (later the Communications Research Centre of the Department of Communications), the National Research Council and other government research organizations across the country. Once a product had been developed, it was tendered to a manufacturing company for production. Where companies did not exist to do the production, they were formed. It was in this manner that Computing Devices and Leigh Instruments, among others, came into being. Leigh Instruments was started with a product called the Crash Position Indicator (CPI), a product they are still making (among others) 30 years later.

The Ottawa Valley was fertile ground for the seeds dropped from the government research organizations. Although most of the electronic products developed were for military and defence use and utilized computer technology, they were still not considered 'real' computers.

In 1957, Computing Devices was given a huge development contract by Atomic Energy of Canada Limited to produce a device that had been designed at the Chalk River laboratories. The device was called the "Kicksorter," a 12-bit core-driven machine which would enable the physicists at Chalk River to do pulse height analysis. According to Denzil Doyle, now president of NABU Manufacturing Ltd. and an employee of Computing Devices in the late 1950s and early 1960s, AECL purchased a large number of these units from Computing Devices from 1957 through to 1963 when they were all replaced by a minicomputer from Digital Equipment.

"For all intents and purposes, all they had to do was add a tiny bit of arithmetic capability to the Kicksorter and it would have been a minicomputer," says Mr. Doyle. "But for some reason or another, the folks at both organizations must have thought of the device as a one-time-only piece of machinery. Although a large number were produced for AECL, I don't think there were any produced for other sales. Perhaps they just didn't see the market potential there."

In the late forties and early fifties the company had attempted to build a computer that had been designed by George Glinski. The original development had taken a great deal of time and it became obvious to those working on it that the machine would be out of date before it was completed.

Computing Devices did enter the computer industry in the late fifties selling an American product called the Bendix G-15. They had begun distributing the military equipment produced by Bendix, and when Bendix got into the computer business, Computing Devices decided to distribute those products as well.

Later, Control Data Corporation in the United States bought out Bendix's U.S. operations. Computing Devices then began representing Control Data equipment in Canada. Many of the people involved there in those early days are still active in the computer industry. Some of these include Mike Goudge, Farrell Chown and Bill Hyndman. David Whiteside, now president of Digital Equipment of Canada Limited, was also with Computing Devices. Eventually, in the late sixties, Computing Devices became a division of Control Data Canada and is today recognized throughout the world as a leader in aerospace technology.

The McBee Company was a subsidiary of a U.S. firm, selling that company's products in Canada. In the late fifties, McBee got into the computer field when it was bought out by Royal Precisions of Montreal with its two computer systems, the LGP-30 and LGP-21. Both were desktop computers with drum memory. Gary Glover, now a senior vice president with Control Data Canada Ltd., was "the only person in McBee who knew what a computer was." When he joined McBee in 1955, the company was totally divorced from the punched card and computer business. But with the Royal Precisions deal, he says he became the instant expert in scientific computing.

"We sold LGP-30s in Sault Ste Marie to Algoma Steel and maintained it by airplane," says Mr. Glover. "And we sold systems to the University of Alberta, the University of Saskatchewan and the University of Montreal. We sold an LGP-30 to Crown Life for their interactuarial department. We went all across the country. Our maintenance policy was that we would maintain equipment within a 50 mile radius of a sales office. So every time we sold one, we had to open up a new office to make the maintenance viable."

Soon afterward, Control Data Corporation bought out Royal Precisions. The market base set up by McBee, Royal Precisions and Computing Devices was the foundation for Control Data Canada in the early sixties.

3

Computing services: The opening of a new dimension

*T*HE COMPUTER SERVICE industry in Canada probably has the highest percentage of Canadian ownership and entrepreneurial activity of all the areas of the computer field, according to Datacrown president Richard G. Taylor. Compared with most high technology industries, its product content—software and services—is much more highly Canadian in origin.

Although this side of the industry began modestly in the mid-1950s, it did not begin to blossom until the mid- to late 1960s.

Clifford Green's Statistical Reporting and Tabulating Ltd. (SRT), formed in 1955 in Toronto, is reputed to be the first independent service centre in Canada. The company's first project was a mail survey conducted for a large advertising agency. The bill for services rendered by SRT was $54—a modest beginning for what has become a $1 billion sector of the computer industry.

In the early years, SRT used IBM unit record equipment. By the late fifties, the company had acquired a Burroughs B283 computer. And in 1964, it added an IBM 360.

Shortly after going into business, Clifford Green called Bell Canada to enquire about a yellow pages listing under a new category, 'Data Processing Services.' "They thought about it for a while and finally told me they'd add that category and list SRT if

I'd take an ad," says Mr. Green. "I bought a half-inch ad and was the only company listed. Today, you'll find hundreds of companies under that heading."

In 1968, poor health, forced Mr. Green to sell SRT, which by then had about 100 employees and revenues of approximately $1 million. Today as president of Business Data Processing Ltd., he is once more active in the industry.

In Vancouver in 1950, a company known today as National Datacentre Corporation (1966) opened its doors under the name of Company Services Limited. The company, run by Geoff Bartlett, has become one of the largest computer service firms on Canada's West Coast.

There were others which had begun as non-computerized firms offering specialized types of services and gradually moving into the computer area. Recording and Statistical Company (R&S), in operation (as Library Bureau) since 1876, offered specialized tabulating and statistical services to insurance companies in Montreal and Toronto. It became a division of Remington-Rand in 1963 through its Toronto operation, and merged into Real Time Datapro in 1971. Its Montreal branch, which used Burroughs equipment, was taken over by Welby Computer Services. That, too, eventually became part of Real Time Datapro.

In Alberta, Prairie Data Processors may have been the first service bureau in Western Canada. It started up in 1959 using an NCR 390 with 100 words of memory and no peripherals.

These firms provided distinctive computational services to a growing number of commercial and scientific clients across the country who couldn't afford to purchase the new and very large computer systems nor hire the staff required to program and operate the systems.

A different kind of computer service was offered by Josef Kates. Dr. Kates began to sever his association with the U of T in 1953. After working on the Trans Canada Airline seat reservation system (see Chapter 1), he formed, with two associates from the University of Toronto Computation Centre the first computer consulting firm in Canada. KCS Data Control Ltd.—for Joe Kates, Len Casciato, Joe Shapiro—began operations in 1954.

"We didn't have even five cents in contracts," Mr. Casciato says. "Each of us put in $750 so that we'd have working capital while we looked for business." The company drew on that capital until about $900 was left. Then revenues started to rise steadily.

As an adjunct to their consulting work, KCS provided computer services, initially by buying time on Ferut, and later on their own IBM 650.

"We used our computer to develop and run big applications that were more of a technical or planning than of a commercial data processing nature," says Dr. Kates. "Most services bureaus supplied accounting or payroll applications. Later we did some of that, but it was never the mainstay of our business. The orientation of the firm was technical, and we went into the more sophisticated, complex type of application, generally known as operations research."

One of the best known of KCS's projects was the development of the world's first and largest computer controlled traffic signal system. "The idea started to generate around the spring of 1957," Len Casciato says. "Joe Kates and I tried to explain to the City of Toronto and Metropolitan Toronto traffic engineers that computers were sufficiently advanced to be used as the central control device for a network of traffic signals. They were both interested and skeptical."

To prove their point, KCS gave a demonstration using an actual traffic signal light connected to their IBM 650 computer. Coloured cards were used to represent automobiles moving in various directions. Persuaded by the demonstration, Metro Toronto Traffic Controller Sam Cass gave KCS the go-ahead for a preliminary study.

In early 1958, KCS presented a report on the feasibility of computer-controlled traffic signals, and agreed, for a quarter of a million dollars, to do an actual pilot study. By 1960, the company was ready to provide an on-the-street demonstration of the system they had devised.

"The demonstration went beautifully," Casciato says. "Even previous detractors were impressed. We got enormously good press, and we were really flying high."

The pilot project continued for a year and a half, without one single mishap. If the computer went down, the fail-safe system was such that control reverted to the former mechanical controllers so smoothly that drivers were unaware that anything had gone wrong. In 1962, a full scale system was approved to control 500 Metro Toronto signals, with some 1,000 traffic detectors connected to the system. The central computer, a Univac 1107 was located in the old Toronto City Hall.

"The Toronto system was not only the world's first, but the world's largest computer controlled traffic system" Len Casciato says. "It has been widely copied, but its capabilities have not been matched anywhere."

In addition to these independent service operations, the multinational companies, such as International Business Machines, Remington-Rand, Burroughs Business Machines, National Cash Register Company, all provided computer services and customized software products to their own hardware clients.

Although each of the multinational centres was important in its own way to its own users, the data centres set up by IBM have had more influence over the character and make-up of the Canadian services industry than any other one factor.

The 705 datacentre, as the installation at Confederation Life Insurance Company was called, was the starting place for junior programmers and applied science representatives such as Mike Howe, Ted White, Dick Taylor and others. They had the guidance of experienced men like Walter Smuk, Jack Kyle, Guy Renfer, Ike Goodfellow and Larry Shick. According to Ted White, (today president of Amdahl Limited in Canada), these people were extremely important in enabling IBM to penetrate the insurance market.

"There was a willingness in the fifties and sixties to experiment and do some pioneering things, primarily in the application area," says Mr. White, "because that was the only area that was open to us. Hence Canada did a lot of leadership things in the large systems area in the life insurance companies, in particular, and in other large organizations such as banks."

During the time that the centre was in operation, the team of IBM programmers created a series of software packages for Confederation Life which were eventually adopted by IBM and marketed to other life insurance companies at home and abroad. Walter Smuk was one of the authors of a package called ALIS (Advanced Life Information System) for Confederation Life, a package which was later instrumental in the formation of the consulting company, SDI Associates, he started with Guy Renfer and David McMullen.

The programs were owned by IBM because they were written by IBM systems people. However, in many cases, they were just given to the customer for whom they were written for a nominal amount. They were then marketed as part of the hardware sale to other customers in the same fields.

"One of the advancements we made in Canada at the 705 centre was something we called the variable length record," says Walter Smuk. "Jack Kyle and I wrote a routine to get around the fixed record length which most computers had in those days. The fixed length was easier to program, but it didn't suit the insurance industry, so we felt we had to come up with something else."

In 1959, with the cancellation of the AVRO aircraft project, A. V. Roe Aircraft Company went out of business. They had had the largest scientific computer available at the time, the IBM 704. It was the only one in Canada then. The computer was suddenly available and IBM decided to keep it for their own use rather than send it back to the United States or try to find another large buyer for the machine. The other alternative was to store it in a warehouse.

The 704 was moved to IBM's offices in Don Mills and the 704 scientific data centre was created. IBM collected together those of its people who were scientifically minded for the centre. Conrad Maheux was put in charge. Others like Ingo Grossman, Helmut Lerch, Mers Kutt and Don Pounder were also there.

"That centre became a very prestigious place to work," says Mr. Grossman. "We did work not only for IBM clients, but also for outside consultants, providing them with capabilities they couldn't get on their own computers. We gained a very high reputation and attracted extremely well-qualified people to work with us. There was no other place quite like it in all of Canada."

Much of the work started by these early computer service companies carried over into the early 1960s. It is difficult to draw a distinct line between the decades. However, the foundation had been laid and the initial construction of a computer services industry had begun.

The education begins

Most of the early industry pioneers, including those mentioned in this chapter, entered computing after studying mathematics or physics. There were no courses in computer science as such.

However, in the fifties, demand for such courses became apparent. At the University of Toronto, Kelly Gotlieb and Pat Hume began teaching extension courses on business applications and, later, graduate level courses on hardware, numerical analysis, etc. About the same time, George Glinski, while president of Computing Devices of Canada, taught computer courses at McGill University and at the University of Ottawa.

In late 1959, the University of Waterloo began to offer computer courses to all engineering students—probably the first university to offer such courses on a wide scale at the undergraduate level.

Dr. Wes Graham, who joined the faculty of the University of Waterloo after five years with IBM, was one of the chief instigators of this program. "At other universities, if there was any computing at all, it was the preserve of graduate students and professors," he says. "I believed that all engineers should know what computers were all about and how to use them. So I talked the university into introducing these courses in 1959 in engineering."

Computing people get together

The data processing associations such as DPMA (Data Processing Managers Association) and CIPS (The Canadian Information Processing Society) had their beginnings in the early days of the computer industry.

In 1947, a group of machine accountants working on unit record systems decided to form a group called the National Machine Accountants Association. "There were four of us at the beginning," says Art Mackey. "There was someone from Canada Wire and Cable, one from Gulf, one from Blue Cross and myself. It was the first users' association."

That NMAA group grew and eventually became DPMA. "The objective of the association was to exchange ideas on how to make something work," says Jim Coverdale, now president of Cover-All Computer Systems, but then an employee of Canadian

National Railways. "There were a lot of innovative people in the group, such as Tom Scrimgeour and Don Barber. In the beginning it was very small, sometimes with only five or six people at the meetings. But an awful lot of good stuff came out of that group."

CIPS had its start, as the Computing and Data Processing Society of Canada, one afternoon in 1958. "Kelly Gotlieb, John Aitchison and I met over lunch one day and decided there were enough people in the computing business to form a computer society," says Ike Goodfellow. "Pat Hume was also involved in the initial stages. When 200 people showed up at the first meeting, that verified our thinking." CIPS was more a society for the scientific and academic users and involved the suppliers. DPMA was strictly a user group.

In retrospect

Looking back on the fifties, Wes Graham says, "All during the late fifties, it was one miracle after another in terms of development, both hardware and software. The tapes got faster and faster, the disks held more and more space, transistors started to show up. I remember when I first saw a random access disk—very impressive. And I remember when magnetic cores came out—they seemed just phenomenal.

"I think of the late fifties as a period of intense excitement. The technology was going ahead in leaps and bounds every year. Each development added a new dimension to computing."

Led by a small group of pioneers, the Canadian computer industry was on its way.

PART TWO

The Sixties

The Selling of the Computer

THROUGHOUT THE SIXTIES, the computer remained enshrouded with the mystique of the incomprehensible, its marvelous secrets understood only by the initiate. However, the power and versatility of this new technology were increasingly apparent in a world swept by social change and turmoil.

The salesman and the entrepreneur were the people who moved the computer into the practical world of business and government.

1

The era of the salesman

*T*HE ERA OF the computer salesman was ushered in at the beginning of the 1960s.

"We went out and marketed our machines to do almost anything," says Honeywell's Pat Suddick. "We talked about the number of people and the amount of money that would be saved and the service that would be rendered. The computer was the panacea for everything."

The major computer users still were the banks, insurance companies, oil companies, manufacturing firms, governments and other large organizations. But the applications of computer technology within those organizations had broadened.

From coast to coast, companies were realizing how useful the new technology could be. The introduction of IBM's transistorized 1401 system in 1959 led to many sales of the system in the early 1960s. Within IBM the 1401 was described as "a computer that the salesman could install himself." That was the expectation, but not quite the reality, according to the salesmen and the systems engineers.

Datacrown's Dick Taylor says he installed the first 1401 in the country at the Texaco (Texas Oil Company) Toronto head office in June 1961. "Texaco was my account as systems engineer," he says, "and on the day of the equipment announcement, Texaco U.S. had ordered a dozen systems and said that one of these systems was coming to Canada.

"The 1401 was very similar to today's microcomputers, although not as reliable," Mr. Taylor continues. "There was no software, as such, and no operating system. I wrote one, in fact, that was nothing by today's standards, but it would load programs—when they were called in—from magnetic tape. I was surprised how many users were prepared to spend the money to justify a magnetic tape just to hold programs."

The 1401 computer systems rented for around $7,000 or $8,000 a month in 1961. They had a lot less computing power than, for example, the present IBM Personal Computer which sells for approximately $8,000 to $9,000 complete with operating system and one application program. However, in 1961, that monthly rental cost was much less than what had been charged for the earlier and larger systems. For the users, it was an attractive and relatively inexpensive way of obtaining in-house data processing power.

These smaller computing systems were also installed in companies like Canadian Oil Companies (known for its White Rose filling stations and sold to Shell Oil in 1966), Shell Oil (which used its 1401 in conjunction with a larger IBM 7070), some of the insurance companies, banks, manufacturers, and commercial businesses. At the same time, IBM was still marketing its other computers, like the 650, one of which was installed at B.C. Hydro in Vancouver in 1960 and another that was programmed to handle the results of the B.C. elections in September, 1960.

In 1963, there were more changes at IBM Canada. Harry Sheppard stepped down as president to become commissioner of the Liquor Control Board of Ontario. Colleagues chaffed him about going "from think to drink."

Jack Brent returned to Canada that year from the IBM U.S. offices to run IBM Canada. He is credited with infusing the organization with a pride in being a Canadian company. He set up the manufacturing division at IBM Canada beginning with the 1401. Mr. Brent remained as president of IBM Canada until 1969, when Bill Moore was appointed to the position.

The other multinationals began earnestly pursuing business all across the country. "IBM and Univac had set up sales and service offices in the major cities west of Ontario by the early 1960s, but the rest of the suppliers had offices only in Toronto," says William C. Hutchison, who joined Honeywell in 1962 as one of its first salesmen and is now one of Canada's leading communications consultants.

"My territory was Western Canada (everything west of Toronto's Yonge Street) for Honeywell. On Monday mornings, I would find myself sitting in the Toronto airport along with the salesmen from General Electric, Burroughs, and NCR. We would all get on the same airplane, heading for Winnipeg. We'd politely chat and ask each other where we were going and what we'd be doing there. And the answer was always the same, 'nothing.' Of course, we were probably following each other to the same accounts in Winnipeg, trying to make a sale. Then we'd end up on the same plane that evening heading for Calgary, telling each other how unsuccessful we'd been. Meanwhile, each of us thought that he had an order with the same company. And so we would follow each other across the country all week, finding ourselves together once more on Friday evening in the Vancouver airport waiting for the flight back to Toronto.

"In those pioneering days, we must have been presenting enough of a threat to IBM to make them finally sit up and notice that we were there," continues Mr. Hutchison. "I think they began to worry that we would start to take their business away from the client base that they had already established, especially in the West.

"Not only were we 'dwarfs' chasing each other across Canada, we now found ourselves being tailed by an IBM vigilante squad. If there was a chance of one of us selling a computer to a client, the IBM 'squad' would descend upon the client to find out why he was going to buy something other than an IBM system and try to talk him out of it—and back into an IBM computer. That squad of top executives from the IBM Toronto head office was very effective in neutralizing a great deal of our activity across the country."

As effective as the IBM vigilante squad was, there were a number of users across Canada who decided to give the newer computer companies and their systems a chance.

"We had been plugging away since 1958, trying to interest users in our equipment," says Honeywell's Pat Suddick. "I realized that we were going to need impressive references to build upon, so we went after the big companies. We also made sure that we had an extremely good group of field service representatives that our clients could depend upon."

Honeywell's first Canadian sale was in 1963 to Bell Telephone for that company's Montreal facility. It was also the first computer that Bell had installed in their operations. (An earlier Honeywell computer had been installed in the Toronto offices of Metropolitan Life Insurance Company in 1958. However, that order had been placed in the U.S. by Metropolitan Life's parent company, with the sale being handled as part of the Honeywell U.S. operations.)

The Honeywell 400 system installed at Bell in 1963 remained in service there until 1979, when it was dismantled and presented to the National Museum of Science and Technology in Ottawa. The nameplate from the computer ("The Honeywell 400 computer—In service at Bell Telephone from 1963 to 1979") is now mounted on a small plaque in Pat Suddick's office in the Honeywell Centre in Toronto. That installation resulted in the sale to the Royal Trust of a similar system (ultimately sold to Bell Telephone as a third system), and in a sale to British American Oil (now Gulf Oil) in Montreal, formerly an entrenched IBM stronghold. The success of these and similar installations put Honeywell in the position of number two computer supplier (after IBM) by the end of the decade.

For the majority of the multinationals, there was a lag of around two years from the time the computer systems were announced in the United States to the time they were available for sale in Canada. As a result, some of the very early installations in Canada were the result of sales through the U.S. operation.

Perhaps the first NCR computers in Canada arrived here this way. NCR 390 computer systems were installed at Prairie Data Processors in Calgary in 1959 and at the Saskatchewan Wheat Pool in 1960. However, that machine was not made available for sale by the Canadian NCR operation until 1962. It was followed by the NCR 310 and 315 models in 1963 and 1964 respectively. One of the latter systems was installed at Eaton's in Toronto in 1964. Unfortunately, there were some problems with the equipment, and Eaton's switched to IBM equipment in the mid-sixties.

Univac lost some ground throughout the sixties, as did Burroughs. It has been said that their marketing strategies did not keep pace with the fine technology they were producing. However, Univac did win out in a severe competition against IBM and Control Data to place their Univac 1107 system in Toronto's (Old) City Hall for the Metropolitan Toronto traffic control application. The system was expected to last 10 years, based on the growth pattern that had been projected for the city's traffic signals. It remained in use until 1982, when it was replaced by a system of distributed micro and minicomputer components. The control panel of the 1107 is to be displayed at the National Museum of Science and Technology.

Prior to the above-mentioned competition, Control Data had not yet established a permanent office in Canada. "The origin of the company in Canada was essentially to try to sell the Control Data 3600 system to the City of Toronto for traffic control," says Gary Glover, now that company's senior vice president of systems and services. "It wasn't until the end of the decade that the company purchased both Computing Devices of Canada and Royal Precisions. In 1967, there were only about 65 people in the whole Canadian organization."

Much of the character of the industry and its competitive aspects were changed by the introduction of the IBM 360 family of computers in 1964. With this announcement, IBM introduced a completely different computer architecture in a series of "compatible" computer systems—through which a user could start with the smallest of the systems, then upgrade as required by adding compatible modules. Peripherals and programs could be interchanged. IBM took a gamble at this time, because it was in fact making its previous equipment obsolete. The idea was to convince existing customers to replace their 650s, 705s, 1401s and 7070s with one of the new models.

"When IBM introduced the 360, they virtually abandoned the 1401," says Pat Suddick of Honeywell, "and that proved to be a small error on their part. They felt they had a large enough grip on the market that they could direct it in any way they wished. They opened up this little slot, a chink in the armor, for the rest of us to slip through. Anyone who had a 1401 had to reprogram and redesign the software systems in order to use a 360. Many of the users were unwilling to do so, and looked around for alternatives.

"Honeywell came out with its 200 system, which was designed to be like a super-1401," continues Mr. Suddick. "We had a system we called the Liberator, to 'liberate' IBM users from the 1401 problems by utilizing a piece of software that would run their programs directly on the Honeywell computer. We sold a multitude of Liberators to replace existing IBM computers. That actually gave us our base of business."

The software aspects of computer use became a priority as the manufacturers attempted to make their systems easier for programmers to use. They began creating languages and packages, which meant that the computer boards no longer had to be rewired to change the programs. Programming instructions were now on magnetic tape.

Most manufacturers supported such commercial languages as Assembler, COBOL (Common Business Oriented Language), FORTRAN (Formula Translator) and RPG (Report Program Generator) in an effort to standardize. However, the manufacturers had their own versions of the languages to work on their own machines. BASIC (Beginner's All-purpose Symbolic Instruction Code) was created somewhat later in the sixties and tended to be used more on the minicomputers than on mainframes.

The new languages facilitated programming and interacting with computers and opened the door for wider use of the systems.

Of course, the languages used up valuable memory space on the computers. This created a need for larger memory units to add on to existing systems. Because IBM had developed a single interface with the 360, companies like Memorex and Storage Technology Corporation were able to build memory units compatible with that interface. Although both companies were started in California, they soon opened Canadian offices to serve the growing market here.

Another outgrowth of the 360 introduction was the beginning of the third party leasing sector of the industry. Companies like Greyhound Computer Leasing, TransAmerica Leasing, G.A.C. Computer Leasing and MAI (Management Assistance Inc.) got their start buying up the 1401, 650 and 705 computers that companies acquiring 360s wanted to dispose of. The computers were then leased to other users who did not want to leave the IBM fold. They rationalized taking two 1401s or multiple 650s at a lower cost (because they were "used" computers) from a leasing firm.

The leasing firms also offered special arrangements to IBM customers who were renting or leasing 360 equipment directly from IBM. Normally, clients were able to apply their rental payments toward the purchase price of the computer from IBM. The computer leasing company would offer to buy the system outright from the customer and lease it back at about 20 per cent less than what was being paid to IBM. To some users, this was an extremely attractive way to obtain a computer without really owning it. People were still concerned about cost justifying the use of computers, and about having large enough applications to warrant the ownership of equipment.

The minicomputer came along to fill the breech.

The minicomputer comes to Canada

The history of the minicomputer in Canada—and indeed in all of North America—is very closely tied in with the history of Digital Equipment Corporation.

In late 1959, a group of scientists at the Massachusetts Institute of Technology (MIT) had developed an 18-bit radar data processing device called the TX-O. Ken Olsen, Stan Olsen, Harold Anderson and Gordon Bell left MIT to set up their own company, Digital Equipment Corporation, to build a commercial form of the TX-O. That computer eventually became the PDP-1 (for Programmed Data Processor).

One of the first PDP-1 systems was sold to the AECL laboratory at Chalk River in 1960 for a real-time, pulse-height-analysis application. AECL decided to purchase another because they wanted to get into a reactor control experiment in 1962. By this time, a new model of the computer (the PDP-4) had been developed, and Digital Equipment recommended that system. AECL agreed, but insisted that a special 12-bit front end would have to be built that would have some intelligence, memory, alarm monitoring capability, level direction and analog to digital (A/D) converter.

According to Denny Doyle, who had just joined Digital in Canada from a position at the Defence Research Board, the AECL project was approximately a $250,000 sale, at a time when Digital on a worldwide basis was doing only about $1.5 million in business. With the prospects of such a large sale, "virtually the whole damn company" descended on Chalk River to assess the situation.

The result was the production of the company's first 12-bit computer, called the PDP-5 by some at Digital and the DC12 (for Digital Controller, 12 bits long) by those who considered it simply a toy not worthy of being called a computer. The PDP-5, created specifically for that application at Chalk River, became a major sales item for Digital Equipment world wide—and the first "minicomputer."

Of course, the machines weren't called minicomputers at the time. "When I opened the doors of Digital Equipment of Canada in 1963, I was really only selling digital modules and some PDP-4s," says Denny Doyle. "The PDP-5 was just coming onstream.

"If you look back to 1963, those were the heady days of nuclear research. Chalk River was booming. The Triumf project in British Columbia (involving the University of British Columbia, University of Victoria, Simon Fraser University, the University of Alberta, and Atomic Energy of Canada Limited) had just been started. The physics market in Canada was extremely strong. So I was able to sell equipment to those physics labs for monitoring and analysis computation as well as data acquisition. I was competing with Hewlett-Packard, which had a digital data acquisition system that also wasn't considered a computer in this market.

"The education market was also very big," Mr. Doyle continues. "In the early 1960s, a number of Colleges of Applied Arts and Technology were opened in Ontario. The CEGEPS (collèges d'enseignement général et professionel) in Quebec, and institutes of technology and community colleges such as SAIT, NAIT, BCIT and Red River Community College also opened across the country. They needed some computing power, but were too small for the mainframe systems that existed then. The 'digital modules' and small systems I had were perfect for that particular market."

Digital Equipment began manufacturing in Canada in early 1964 through a strange set of circumstances, according to Mr. Doyle. "Ken Olsen had heard that John Leng, who had been with AECL in Chalk River when the original PDP-5 sale had gone through, was considering manufacturing digital modules in Canada and was looking for venture capital to do so.

"He (Olsen) called me in and said, 'If anyone is going to manufacture digital modules in Canada, I think it should be us. So why don't you hire John Leng and see if you can talk him into putting together a manufacturing plant.' I hired John as manufacturing manager, then went out to Carleton Place and bought an old woolen mill (because the first Digital plant in Massachusetts was in an old woolen mill), and we started hiring other people."

Ken Olsen may have suggested the idea of Digital Equipment manufacturing in Canada, but Denny Doyle is credited with being responsible for making DEC a good corporate citizen, and the second largest computer firm in Canada. He has untiringly championed the cause that companies doing business in Canada should have assets invested in the country and should also be conducting research and development on products to suit this country's needs.

In the United States, a number of small firms followed in Digital's wake, producing similar 12-bit digital machines. Most of them also entered the Canadian marketplace, selling their systems through distributors or representatives. One of these U.S. firms, Scientific Data Systems, sold its SDS 910 (a 12-bit machine) through Instronics in Canada. SDS was eventually bought out by Xerox Corporation in 1970.

Another U.S. firm, Computer Control Corporation, became part of the Honeywell organization in 1966. Its DDP116 system, one of the first 16-bit computers developed, became the Honeywell 816 minicomputer. According to Honeywell's Pat Suddick, "The takeover was one of the important steps in the deployment of the same technology to all areas of the company (Honeywell). At the same time, microprocessors were being incorporated in process control, missile guidance systems and the like. Since then, they've become a major element in the concept of distributed data processing systems, on which so much of the company's future is built."

Hewlett-Packard (Canada) Ltd. opened an office in Montreal in 1961 to market its electronics machinery, which included at that time an audio oscillator and some data acquisition equipment. The first HP computer, an instrumentational computer to work with other HP instruments, was introduced in 1966. Although the company has since diversified and expanded its product line and has become the 12th largest computer firm in Canada (and the third largest minicomputer supplier in the country), it has remained strictly a sales and service operation here, with all manufacturing done in the United States.

Data General (Canada) Inc., whose senior management in the U.S. came directly from Digital Equipment Corporation, began operations here in late 1969. The company set up its head office in Hull, Quebec, along with a short-lived manufacturing facility. The plant was originally designed to manufacture the company's Nova minicomputers to serve the Canadian market. It was later recognized that the operation was not cost-effective, and the facility was closed. Since that time, Data General has expanded its sales and field engineering locations across Canada, relying on the U.S. parent for its hardware and software products.

Digital Equipment of Canada is still the only multinational minicomputer firm manufacturing in this country.

The minicomputer (apparently dubbed such by John Leng of Digital Equipment because of the success of the mid-sixties mini-skirt phenomenon) utilizes microprocessor-based technology that was under development at that time.

Even the large scale computer manufacturers such as IBM, Control Data, NCR, Burroughs and Sperry Univac began incorporating the new semiconductor technology into their equipment, thus creating their own minicomputers to compete on an effective level for the small business computer market.

However, the minicomputer "revolution" can be traced back to the early efforts of Denny Doyle and Digital Equipment. "I suppose I was really Digital's first customer in Canada, with the orders for digital modules I placed with the U.S. office while I was working at the Defence Research Board," says Mr. Doyle.

"When I started selling the modules myself, I got a lot of support from people like Bob Andrews at Canadian General Electric in Peterborough. That company was building nuclear reactor fuelling systems, and Bob called me in one day to design a computer system to do the job. They had been considering purchasing an IBM 1800, but Bob felt my equipment would do a better job. I got the contract for about $100,000 worth of modules and the prospect of a system worth half a million dollars.

"That led to another very large contract with the Interprovincial Pipeline Company through Harvey Gellman and Mike Holt (who had been the IBM salesman working on the CGE Peterborough account)," Doyle continues. "Harvey had got a contract to do the modelling work on the interprovincial pipeline, and Mike was working with him at that time. They had been using an IBM 360 in Edmonton and wanted Harvey to recommend some equipment to be used at each pumping station to gather data. Mike called me, remembering the system I had designed for CGE, and I got the contract to supply some 25 station computers for the pipeline."

Contracts such as these provided a solid customer base and a good reputation for Digital Equipment. They also provided a foundation upon which the whole minicomputer industry was able to build, and from which the microcomputer industry has developed.

2

Canada
builds its own computer

ALTHOUGH MOST OF the technical innovations in the computer field originated in the United States, the ground that had been broken by enterprising Canadian computer groups in the fifties began to yield rich harvests in the 1960s.

At Ferranti-Packard in Toronto, work began on a computer that would make history as a top-quality machine designed, developed, engineered and built in Canada—the general purpose FP 6000.

Ted Strain, who joined Ferranti in 1960 and is now president of ESE Limited, describes the events that led to the development of the first FP 6000.

"We had a group of people at Ferranti who knew how to design computers. We also had a hot-shot salesman who was dispatched down to the Federal Reserve Bank in New York. In the fifties, we'd installed a special purpose cheque sorting machine, and now the bank wanted to upgrade the equipment. The Ferranti salesman recommended the use of a general purpose computer, and said we could design and build one to run the sorting machine.

"The customer signed on the dotted line, the salesman came back to Toronto with the order, and were in the computer business.

The result was the FP 6000, the first 'time-sharing," multitasking machine in the world. The multi-tasking feature enabled several jobs to be run simultaneously, each protected from the others, and all sharing the resources of the central processing unit and peripherals. This feature was a significant technological breakthrough, preceding similar capabilities later introduced in the equipment of other manufacturers.

Fred Longstaff was the architect of the FP 6000 hardware. With two others, he also wrote the Fortran compiler. The logic was designed by Ted Strain. Most of the software was produced by "Ian Sharp and his merry men." (The epithet is Mr. Longstaff's).

Irish-born Ian Sharp had joined Ferranti from England in 1960 as chief programmer. To the company he brought his software expertise and, according to colleagues, an irreverent, puckish sense of humor and a sometimes acerbic tongue.

Although some of the players had changed, the Ferranti team continued to perform brilliantly. In 1965, the Federal Reserve Bank took delivery of the FP 6000 to run their cheque sorting machine. Additional FP 6000s were subsequently built and installed at the Toronto Stock Exchange, the Saskatchewan Power Corporation and the Naval Research Establishment in Dartmouth, Nova Scotia. Technologically advanced Canadian-built computers were moving into the marketplace.

But not for long. In 1964, the British government, alert to the potential impact of electronic equipment, moved to consolidate the nation's computer industry. International Computers and Tabulators Ltd. (ICT) was designated as the centralized vehicle through which Britain would compete world wide with Univac, IBM and other major computer manufacturers. One of the companies purchased by ICT (which later became ICL, International Computers Limited), was Ferranti. The FP 6000 design rights, hardware and software were included in the sale. In Canada, Ferranti-Packard was out of the computer business.

On the basis of the FP 6000, ICL developed the 1900 series, marketing billions of dollars' worth of computers around the world. "I took great vicarious delight in seeing ICL sell hundreds and hundreds of computers based on the FP 6000 design," Fred Langstaff comments wryly.

The Ferranti team disbanded. Don Ritchie, Fred Longstaff, Ted Strain, Gord Lang and some of the other engineers formed ESE

Limited in 1964. According to Mr. Longstaff, "We all raised our hands and swore a solemn oath never again to develop a general purpose computer." The first product was a delay equalizer for CN/CP Telecommunications. ESE has since become a major distributor, designer and producer of data communications switches and modems.

Ian Sharp and eight colleagues formed I.P. Sharp Associates Ltd., a software company offering time sharing facilities. "We had published a fair amount about what we were doing in software design at Ferranti-Packard and had given papers at computer conferences," Mr. Sharp says. "There was a healthy respect for what we were doing in the industry.

"I got several phone calls from other computer manufacturers interested in acquiring the entire software development group. So we decided to set up shop ourselves and see if we could make a go of it."

Not only did he "make a go of it," Ian Sharp established a timesharing network that would expand to include users in more than 30 countries throughout the world.

In the sixties, however, early contracts were with ICL, Univac and IBM. The last involved work on the implementation of Dr. Kenneth Iverson's A Programming Language (APL).

APL had been conceived in the late fifties by Dr. Iverson, who is a native of Camrose, Alberta. Tall, lanky, informal, he looks like a university professor, which indeed he was at one time. As a faculty member at Harvard University, he developed a special mathematical notation that he used in teaching to describe and analyze data processing applications. In 1960, he joined IBM, and from 1964 to 1967 worked with a group that included Dr. Adin Falkoff, Roger Moore and others, to develop a computer implementation of APL. In 1980, Dr. Iverson received the ACM Turing award for technical contributions to the computer industry.

To Ian Sharp, APL looked like "a good way to implement applications programming." He credits Roger Moore as the "technical brains behind the company." Mr. Moore, he says, made APL work and implemented the timesharing system under which it ran.

In August, 1969, I.P. Sharp Associates' first customers signed on to the timesharing system from Ottawa, Toronto, and Washington. It was the beginning of a network that in the seventies would include users in North America, Europe, and Australia.

A second chance for Canada

In the 15 years since Consolidated Computer Inc. began operations, controversy has dogged both the company and its officials.

The company was started in 1967 in Kingston, Ontario, by Mers Kutt and Don Pamenter, who had both come out of the Honeywell ranks. Mr. Kutt had been approached by Queen's University to set up a computing centre. Since computer science at the time was under the jurisdiction of the math department, he was given a professor's appointment as well.

"My arrangement was that I be allowed to set up my own company in parallel," says Mr. Kutt, "without jeopardizing my position in the department. I had already developed the idea of a key-to-drum product and wanted to bring such a product to the marketplace. Don also had the idea of starting a small service operation for computerizing doctors' accounting procedures.

"So we started a company called Consolidated Computer Services, buying time on the Queens' computer. Royal Trust had a manual service for the application that had run into some problems. Our service was computerized and running well. The executives at Royal Trust were impressed with what we did and helped to find financing for Consolidated. By the fall of 1968 we had secured about a half a million dollars in private placements. The following summer we went public."

By the time the company went public, it had developed its own timesharing service based on a Hewlett-Packard computer to which some new hardware had been added. The turnkey timesharing system was sold to customers who would then hook into the CCI main computer.

But Consolidated Computer had also entered the manufacturing field, with its Key-Edit key-to-drum data entry computer. That system utilized a Digital Equipment PDP-8 minicomputer to which drums (from Vermont Research Corporation) and other hardware components were added. The software for the system was created by Consolidated.

Because most of the parts for the Key-Edit system were

manufactured by other firms, it has been said that Consolidated Computer was not really a computer manufacturer, but strictly a computer assembly firm. Mers Kutt does not agree, stating that the printed circuit board used in the system, the keyboard, and numerous other small parts were indeed manufactured in Canada by Consolidated itself.

"We were definitely building our own terminals right from the start. And we were ahead of our time on a number of ideas. Having one board with as much logic on it as possible was somewhat unconventional at the time, but it's exactly what Apple and others did many years later. The Key-Edit was, I believe, a rather radical piece of equipment for its time. The software we created was quite complex. We were servicing each keystroke of every operator on the system. I think there's some good technology that was applied."

It was the first time that hardware manufacturing on any level had been undertaken in Canada since the computer division of Ferranti-Packard had closed in 1964. By the time manufacturing had begun, Consolidated Computer had moved its head offices to Toronto.

In June 1969, the product was demonstrated at the DPMA exhibition held that year in Montreal. The system was not quite ready for manufacture, but it did work, according to Mr. Kutt. "The convention hall was hot, and the air conditioning wasn't very good. So we brought in buckets of ice and put them inside the back of the computer to keep the temperature down low enough so that the machine would work. We had four girls keying information through the show, and the unit didn't break down once.

"I think we were the first anywhere to exhibit such equipment at a public showing," continues Mr. Kutt. "There were other people who had independently developed key-to-disk type products, but we were being picked as the company that had the right margins, the right package together. We even had a report done on us by Arthur D. Little, commissioned by someone in the United States."

The future looked bright for Consolidated Computer. William G. Hutchinson had come on board in 1969 as marketing manager. Systems had been sold abroad (in England and in the

United States). There was a great deal of interest in the product in Europe. Major sales of equipment were also recorded in Canada, to companies like General Motors. And research into future product lines was under way. It looked as though Canada were finally on the map with an independent computer manufacturer. However, more difficult times were ahead for Consolidated Computer Inc.

Canadian university activities

At the University of Toronto computing centre, the pace of activities quickened with the acquisition in 1961 of an IBM 7090 processor. To pay for the machine, the U of T for the first time in its history issued a cheque for more than $1 million.

With the installation of what was then, according to Kelly Gotlieb, the only large-scale computer in Canada, the university began to sell a substantial amount of computing time. Eventually, more than a million dollars' worth of time was purchased by users, including organizations such as Imperial Oil and Ontario Hydro.

The 7090, Dr. Gotlieb adds, was a "tremendous workhorse of a machine—very reliable. We drove it night and day for years, until 1976."

Although in the early sixties the U of T had Canada's only large-scale computer, other universities across the country began developing their own computer facilities and centres.

In 1957, the University of British Columbia's ALWAC was the second computer to be installed in a Canadian university. The ALWAC was succeeded by an IBM 1620 and an IBM 7040 in the sixties.

The University of Calgary's data centre was built around an IBM 360/50 processor. At the University of Alberta, an LGP-30 was followed by an IBM 1620 and later by an IBM 7040/1401 system. In 1967, the university further upgraded to an IBM 360/67.

The University of Montreal installed Control Data equipment for its computing requirements. The University of Ottawa had an IBM 360/65.

By the end of the sixties, machines were installed in most

universities to handle their own computer requirements, and many sold time to business and government users as well.

However, perhaps the most dramatic development occurred at the University of Waterloo, which in the fifties had pioneered the teaching of computer science courses to all engineering students.

By 1965, computer science had emerged from its original status as a division of the mathematics department into a separate department in the university. About the same time, Waterloo introduced a co-operative system of education. Students could study for four months, and then put their newly acquired knowledge to practical use by working for four months.

Computer Science Days for high school students were also initiated. On Saturdays and every day during Christmas and Easter breaks, thousands of high school students from across Ontario began pouring into the University of Waterloo for a one-day course in computing.

In addition, the university started to produce software programs which were used as educational tools at Waterloo and were marketed outside the university both nationally and internationally.

The driving force behind this sustained innovative activity was Dr. Wesley Graham, former applied science representative for IBM. Wes Graham, whose youthful face and effervescent enthusiasm belie his silver hair, has spent more than 20 years working with his students and for Waterloo.

When the co-operative program was introduced, he traveled across Ontario, visiting large companies throughout the province to persuade them to hire Waterloo co-op students. "I tried to explain to them that it would be to everyone's best interest to have good computing people trained, and that they should give these students a chance," Dr. Graham says. "Now companies line up to hire our students."

He adds that initially there was fairly widespread criticism of the co-op program. It was called "very unacademic." Some said Waterloo was "not really a university. Imagine students working, instead of just thinking!"

Dr. Graham is proud of the achievements of Waterloo students and graduates.

"It's different at Waterloo," he says. "It's really different from a lot of places. Every piece of educational software that has been created here has been created by students, not professors. I think Waterloo has been innovative and our products have been successful because they have been developed to solve actual problems that we faced at Waterloo. We had to solve them to survive. Other people have the same problems and need solutions, too."

One of the first and most widely known programs produced at the University of Waterloo in the early sixties was WATFOR (Waterloo Fortran). Developed by four third-year students, WATFOR significantly increased the speed at which Fortran programs could be processed. "If the computer could handle a student job in two minutes, WATFOR enabled the machine to do it in a second," Dr. Graham says. "So in two minutes we could do 100 jobs instead of one. That meant we could really teach a lot of computing at Waterloo."

WATFOR was followed by WATFIV (Waterloo Fortran IV), WATBOL (Waterloo Cobol) and dozens of other programs. In 1972, Paul Dirksen, now director of Waterloo's computing services, and Paul Cress, then senior systems analyst at SDL, won the ACM Grace Murray Hopper award for their creation of the WATFOR compiler while students at Waterloo. By the eighties, more than 50 Waterloo software products were being distributed by some 3,000 user organizations around the world.

Dr. Graham also played a part in the university's acquisition of leading-edge computer facilities. "In 1965 we had a bit of luck," he explains. "By that time it was clear that we needed a building for our computing activities, and we needed much bigger computer equipment. I suggested that we build a $7 million building and install $5 million of computer equipment.

"What I was proposing was outrageous, really. We were a small university, not even 10 years old, with hardly any buildings on campus and only about 4,000 students. And I was suggesting facilities bigger than those in any university in North America.

"We told the provincial government what we wanted—Bill Davis was Minister of Education at that time—and I'll be damned if we didn't get it!"

The repercussions, he says, were felt across North America. Waterloo, with a newly installed IBM 360/75, became the biggest computing establishment in Canada. Immediately, other universities in Ontario began demanding government support for their computer facilities.

"We started getting visitors from places like Stanford and Cornell and UCLA," Dr. Graham says. "And we started reading about this place in Waterloo, and how imaginative and courageous the government was to support it. The decision to support Waterloo had a positive impact on computing at universities all across North America."

Software to the fore

According to Wes Graham, "One thing we really can do in Canada is to develop software—that's a business we're very good at."

The software developed at Waterloo is one example of that Canadian ability. The contributions of Ken Iverson and of Ian Sharp's organization, mentioned earlier in this chapter, have earned international recognition.

Other examples can be cited. Frank Van Humbeck's work in designing operating system software for the IBM 1710 system is still remembered by members of the industry.

"In the sixties, Frank was working with the paper mill industry," a colleague recalls. "The standard IBM operating system product was not adequate to do the required job, so he wrote one that was. He had a lot of influence on the design of the operating system of the next generation of IBM computers."

A product called Extracto was developed in the late sixties by Jacques Roy when he was working with a Quebec consulting and computer services firm, Aquila-BST. M. Roy left the company and formed Optipro, Inc. in Montreal to continue the development of software products.

Extracto is a simple language that enables a user with no previous computer training to extract data from a file, manipulate the data (by addition, multiplication, etc.) and specify output report format. The software has been used in more than 500 installations throughout the world.

A Calgary firm, Data-Man Ltd. (part of DMC Information Systems Ltd.), was formed in 1968 as a system software firm by two "easterners" and an Englishman. Sam Clarke, John Bowden, and Clive Pringle created a data retrieval, file management, and report generation system they named Data-Man for use on IBM 360 computer systems. That software product is now also sold in the United States through a subsidiary, and in Europe through a distributor. Data-Man Ltd. is one of the largest and most successful software companies in Canada.

Much more innovative software work has been done in Canada, by both large and small software houses and by the multinational hardware firms as well.

Software creativity has given many Canadian companies the opportunity to export their expertise—and a chance to try to balance the deficit created by the importation of computer hardware.

3

Computing services move ahead

THROUGHOUT THE SIXTIES, computing services began to blossom as entrepreneurs recognized the potential of selling computer time, specialized services, and software programs to companies without in-house computer systems.

The entrepreneurs came from various computer suppliers and commercial businesses that were computer users. However, the majority had worked for IBM Canada Ltd. With about 70 per cent of the computer hardware market, IBM had installed the lion's share of computers across the country. Entrepreneurs felt this sector of the user community might benefit most from computer services offered on an outside IBM computer, or from software services for their in-house systems.

Although not a computer service firm *per se,* Precision Data Card deserves mention here as the first offshoot from the giant IBM Canada corporation. Peter Ely and Dan Owen decided to venture forth from the IBM fold in 1962, at a time when the idea seemed somewhat of a folly.

"I was installing some IBM equipment in a downtown Toronto location," says Peter Ely, "and there were some people from Chicago there while we were working. We started talking about the various supplies needed for the system, which as a matter of course were sold to the customer by IBM.

"One of the people from Chicago said that these supplies were available from outside sources in the United States and that customers didn't have to buy them from IBM. That led to further discussions and Dan Owen and I decided to form our own company to sell computer supplies—in particular punch cards."

Mr. Ely and Mr. Owen gathered funds from private sources ("mainly our wives' bank accounts") and also borrowed from the Industrial Development Bank (now the Federal Business Development Bank) to set up Precision Data Card in Toronto.

"We were the first IBM employees to quit the company to start up our own firm," says Mr. Ely. "Some of the others thought we were a pretty strange breed and were convinced that we would drown. IBM was quite fair about the whole situation. They mentioned that selling punch cards was a risky venture, because they would soon be replaced by other media, but didn't try to talk us out of leaving. IBM gave us stiff competition, but never once tried anything underhanded."

By 1964, Precision Data Card had established a branch in London, England, and two years later one in Montreal. The name was changed to Precision Data Company in 1967 and the product line was expanded to include magnetic tape, computer ribbons, disk packs, and a magnetic tape evaluation service. The company also acquired a subsidiary of a U.S. firm in Winnipeg, National Checking Company Ltd., and opened a branch in Vancouver. Manufacturing of a magnetic tape cleaner was begun in Toronto.

Precision Data Company was sold to Control Data Canada in the spring of 1970 and became the Precision Data Division (later called the Business Products Division). Peter Ely and Dan Owen were invited to join Control Data to run the division, but both declined and left the computer industry altogether to pursue other interests.

"Being the first, we set an example for others within IBM," says Peter Ely. "They saw that it was possible to go out and compete head on with IBM and survive."

"In the fifties and early sixties, IBM had a very entrepreneurial attitude," says Amdahl's Ted White. "At the datacentres, we were building life insurance systems and banking systems. There was a lot of scope for individual creativity. And a lot of creative people came up from those ranks. When IBM decided to get out of the creativity business, those particular people left and went out on their own."

IBM went out of the "creativity business" with the introduction of the 360 family of computers in 1964 and the decision to unbundle its software in 1969. Not only did these two factors open the doors for other hardware suppliers to move and acquire more of the hardware business, it also paved the way for entrepreneurs to begin selling the software and services that IBM would no longer offer as part of the hardware purchase price.

In the very early sixties, a number of small companies were formed to provide consulting and software services, often renting or borrowing computer time from large user installations. These service firms were located across Canada to serve local or regional areas.

In the Canadian West, the computer services activity in the early 1960s became more specialized as companies were formed to process information for the petroleum industry, other resource industries and commercial clients.

Computrex Centres Limited was started by Mart Kernahan and William Taylor in Calgary in 1960 using an LGP-30 computer system. The company introduced digital plotting to Canada in 1962. In 1965, the first digitizer system for oil industry service was added. Today, Computrex has nine branches across Canada and is a leading supplier of computer graphics, plotting systems and services, computer output microfilm (COM) and computer input microfilm (CIM) services and equipment, along with micropublishing.

West Coast Electronic Data Processing Ltd. was formed in 1963 in Victoria, B.C., by Earl Large to offer specialized accounting services. The name was changed in 1969 to Datatech Systems Ltd. and the service offerings were expanded to include consulting, software development, third party (OEM) sales of minicomputer equipment, and maintenance of those systems. With branches in British Columbia and Alberta, Datatech is one of the largest data processing companies in western Canada.

Datamation Centres came into being in 1965 with the merger of Prairie Data Processors of Calgary and an Edmonton firm, Datamation, which had been founded by Bory Margolus. Both were equipped with Honeywell 200 computer systems. The new owners, Englishman Doug Irving and Canadian Doug Mitchell, created a company known for its in-depth knowledge and expertise in the area of accounting systems. They expanded in 1970 through an affiliation with Winnipeg-based Symbionics Ltd. Datamation's Edmonton operation was sold to R. Angus Computer Services in 1971, and the Calgary sector was bought by Nu-West Development Corporation and incorporated as Data-mation (1971) Ltd.

In Vancouver, the University of British Columbia in particular played a major role in the computing services field, renting time on its mainframe system to many small specialized service firms. That connection provided the impetus in the late sixties and early seventies for more small firms to enter the field.

Ontario becomes the hub

Ontario, especially Toronto, became the centre of most of the computing services activity during the sixties. The new data centres and software service suppliers needed to be near the head office sites of both user and computer supplier organizations that were located in the province. The data communications services that would be offered in the seventies would change that somewhat, but for now services had to be where the users were. As well, a high percentage of qualified professionals knowledgeable in data processing were located in Ontario— many in the user and supplier companies.

Some of the computing services companies formed during this period have gone on to become national organizations with a central computer site at their head office location and branch offices in every major population centre across the country. Others are now international firms offering services to clients outside Canada through a centrally-located computer site in Canada. Still others have remained small or medium sized facilities serving strictly a local market, while a few have since merged with larger service firms. Whatever their destiny, their beginnings are an indication of the intense activity that pervaded the data processing industry during the sixties.

KCS was the largest company offering specialized computing and operations research services at the time. Early in 1967, the consulting part of the organization, which made up the largest part of the business, merged with the Toronto-based consulting firm Peat, Marwick to form Kates, Peat, Marwick. The services sector of the company was eventually sold to Consumers' Gas. Dr. Kates is now president of Josef Kates Associates, Inc. of Toronto, a firm that provides traffic and systems consulting services.

I.P. Sharp Associates Ltd., as mentioned in a previous chapter, was founded in 1964 by Ian Sharp when Ferranti's computer division folded.

Commercial and Technical Services Ontario (trademark Comtech) had been founded in 1964 to develop customized systems for various companies on Honeywell equipment. In 1965, Donald M. McPhail came in as president of the firm directly from the management consulting firm of Urwick Currie (now Coopers & Lybrand). The company developed its Paymaster payroll system in 1968 and began specializing in the financial accounting area, marketing services primarily to small and medium sized companies.

Until 1969, Comtech operated as a private company. That year it made a reverse takeover of a public company called Fibre Products Ltd., which made automobile seats. However, the company was bought back by Don McPhail in the mid-seventies. The new company, Comtech Group International Limited, is one of the top 15 computing service companies in Canada. A public company, its shares are traded on the Toronto Stock Exchange.

Through the years, Comtech has expanded, opening research and development facilities in southern Ireland, acquiring a computerized bookkeeping service (Telaccount Ltd.), becoming a third party supplier for Digital Equipment minicomputers which it connects by normal telephone lines from the client's offices to high-speed computers in Comtech's network. The company now backs up its service with a full range of applications and software developed in its own research facilities.

Three ex-IBM systems engineers set out in 1965 to form a specialized consulting firm, AGT Management Systems. Gerry Wanless, Helmut Lerch, and Ingo Grossman formed the company to provide services for applications that were "outside the capability of human beings to do without computing equipment," according to Ingo Grossman. "There were new things happening in mathematics that would never have happened if there were no computers, such as linear programming," says Helmut Lerch.

AGT was one of the first software houses to be formed in Canada. When it started in 1965, the only other firms in that field were KCS and Harvey Gellman & Associates. With the mathematical and analytical background of Messrs. Lerch and Grossman, and the reputations they had gained from their work at the IBM 704 scientific data centre, AGT set out to specialize in large detailed projects. One of the first assignments, and the one Ingo Grossman feels put AGT "on the map as a significant force in Canadian services," was a contract in 1965 with the Ontario Ministry of Health for a computer program to handle the newly formulated Ontario Medical Services Insurance Plan (OMSIP), now known as the Ontario Health Insurance Plan (OHIP).

"We were given the mission of preparing the organization that would process all of OMSIP as well as its computer system," says Helmut Lerch. "We not only had to design the system, we also had to go through the whole computer selection process. The regulations hadn't even been worked out. We started talking with them in November, 1965, and the system was expected to go live on April 1, 1966.

"They wanted to have the first few thousand welfare recipients on the plan by April ... everybody on welfare in Ontario was automatically covered. The organization that would administer the health plan had to grow from zero to 600 staff and they were expected to process about 20,000 medical claims a day. It was a tall order, but we managed to do it, and on time."

AGT continued doing this type of consulting and software work until 1968 when Gerry Wanless decided that the future was going to be in the service bureau business, not in consulting. He wanted to change the structure and direction of AGT and bring Ted White on board as a fourth partner. Helmut Lerch and Ingo Grossman wanted to keep the company as it was, so Gerry Wanless and Ted White formed a computing services firm called Dataservice. They felt there was a great deal of goodwill associated with the AGT name and concluded a deal to buy the shares held by Grossman and Lerch. The company name was changed to AGT Data Services, with Ted White and Gerry Wanless as the principal shareholders. Helmut Lerch stayed on with the company until 1969 as its technical director, while Ingo Grossman decided to "retire" from the data processing field. (That retirement lasted only three years—until 1971—at which time Lerch and Grossman again teamed up to form Versa Management Systems, a consulting firm along the same lines as the original AGT.)

The focus of the new AGT was on identifying various market opportunities, then developing products and services to meet those markets. Mr. Wanless and Mr. White did not want to sell only computer cycles. So they also created software systems for five business areas that had highly differentiated products and that were not presently being served by anyone else in the computer industry. Some of the software products included Keydata for small distributors and manufacturers, Fundservice for mutual fund and RRSP functions, and other financial packages for brokerage and investment firms. "Our feeling was that once we had the software, we could be somewhat isolated from competition," says Mr. White. The new company had gone public soon after it opened, possibly the first software house to do so in Canada. It managed to survive the shakedown of the computer stock market at the end of the decade.

Two other ex-IBM salesmen, Barry Consiglio and Bill Wood, founded EDP Industries Inc. in 1966. The Toronto firm used Honeywell equipment in its datacentre, providing stiff competition for firms such as Cover-All and Comtech. EDP was eventually sold to interests in Vancouver, where it continues today to offer accounting data processing services and related software products.

SDI Associates

Also in 1966, Walter Smuk, Guy Renfer, and David McMullen got together to form SDI Associates, a consulting and software firm that would supply services to the life insurance industry. All three had worked with IBM on several projects with large Canadian life insurance companies such as London Life, Manufacturers Life, Great West Life, and others. Their backgrounds, experiences, and goals were similar enough for them to decide to form their own company.

Soon after SDI had started up, the three partners were joined by more ex-IBMers like Ray Demers (who came to represent the firm in Quebec), Richard Taylor, Tony Simms, Bruce Campbell and others. They financed the organization by personally contributing about $10,000 each. "But we still had very little capital," says Walter Smuk. "All of us went way down in salary from what we had been earning at IBM, because we weren't sure how we could justify larger salaries for what we were about to do. We opened up a small office on St. Clair Avenue West and decided that rather than purchasing or leasing a computer ourselves, we would try to work out an arrangement to rent time on a large user organization's computer. We finally struck a bargain with

Lever Brothers and found ourselves working midnights at their facilities doing the debugging and programming of the systems we were creating for customers.

"We did some consulting to IBM on the ALIS life insurance system that I had helped develop (at Confederation Life)," Smuk continues. "In fact, our first cheque was for $100 from IBM Canada. Then we were introduced into other companies we had come to know through association with IBM.

"The following year, we were approached by a group of five British life insurance companies to explore the possibility of setting up the equivalent of a computing centre supporting the companies in Canada. We gave them a proposal. It started out as a consulting assignment that led to a total project development. They then asked us to run the datacentre for them with a small keypunching group. That led to our offering the facilities management service to other life insurance firms, along with the generalized life insurance program we had developed. That turned out to be the software package that put SDI on its feet."

Cover-All Computer Services

Cover-All Computer Services is a somewhat unique small success story in that the company's founder came from a user rather than a supplier background. Jim Coverdale had worked in the accounting departments of Canadian National Railways, General Wire and Cable, and Foundation Company, and had been introduced to data processing in these positions. He started Cover-All in 1966 as a one-man operation to provide accounting data processing services.

In the beginning, he brokered time on an IBM 360 computer at Sun Oil Company, working through the night when the computer wasn't being used and often putting in 18 hours or more each day to get the work done. He found other 360 sites willing to broker time as well. "We had keys to probably half a dozen buildings in Toronto that I could get into through the night at any time to let people in and see that they got organized," says Coverdale. "Some companies had a great fear of letting anybody into their installations and because a lot of the equipment was new, you had to know how to move from one installation to another and how to change the JCL (job control language), how to apply the operating system so that the system would simply run."

As the operation grew, the brokering died off. The service bureau applications built up and the Cover-All staff continued to buy batch shift time, running the midnight shift until about 1971 when they bought a Univac 9400 computer and set up their own installation. However, during the first year, the computer was left in the Univac offices, with Univac buying back some time on the machine for demonstrations. Nine years later, Cover-All moved back to IBM equipment with a 370 computer system, and also began using Digital Equipment minicomputers.

A small-to-medium sized firm with revenues hovering around $3 million to $4 million, Cover-All does most of its business in southern Ontario, although it does have an office in Edmonton through a subsidiary company. While "almost every one of the companies that were in business" when Cover-All was starting up have now been sold or have gone out of business, Cover-All has managed to keep going. "I guess the main reason for our staying in business has been the ability to provide good service," says Coverdale. "We have a lot of people who are practical, who have a good deal of accounting knowledge. We work in the accounting area and our people give advice and help that has nothing to do with computers."

Quebec in ferment

The "Quiet Revolution" in Quebec left ample room for innovation in the computer service field. The Société de Mathématiques Appliquées was created in 1965 by a group of professors from the University of Montreal. The group had established a reputation for technical competence with their work in acoustical design for the Place des Arts in Montreal. They began with systems development and toward the end of the sixties started to provide other computer services as well, using a Control Data 6600 mainframe.

Among their specialities was the development of software packages for hospitals and health services. They also designed the numbering system for the Quebec Medicare.

About 1970 SMA went public and the stock was well received on the market.

However, in the early seventies, the company experienced financial difficulties. Industry observers say that perhaps the difficulties occurred because the principals' technical skills were greater than their management skills. In addition, they may have been handicapped by the fact that their Control Data computer was not IBM-compatible. In 1972, SMA was acquired by the Power Corp.

Also in Quebec, two complementary service companies merged in 1969 to form Aquila-BST, which was for a time one of the largest and most profitable service operations of its kind in Canada.

Aquila Services Ltd. had for several years been providing computer services in Quebec. One of the founders was John O'Brien, an anglophone IBM graduate from the Montreal office.

BST (Paul Berthiaume, Simon St. Pierre and Robert Thériault) et Associés had been providing consulting services since 1966. The company had experienced spectacular growth, increasing from a staff of five in January 1967 to 65 by mid-1969.

"We were the second consulting firm established in Quebec, probably the third in Canada," says Gaston Beauséjour, who joined BST in 1967 and in 1969 became vice president and director of the data processing centre of Aquila-BST. "Among our projects was the implementation of the online Montreal stock exchange system."

Shortly after the two companies merged, Aquila-BST required funds for expansion. A controlling interest was sold to Edper Investments Ltd., Montreal, who were eager to get into the lucrative high technology area.

However, Edper's interest in technology stock was short lived, and in 1970 control of Aquila-BST was acquired by an American firm, Computing and Software.

"Berthiaume left immediately to go into politics and became a state minister," M. Beauséjour recalls. "When they had fulfilled their management contracts, St. Pierre became executive vice president of the Olympics' organizing committee, and Thériault created a distributorship for telecommunications equipment. I went to the Quebec Treasury Board as director of data processing."

Later, in the seventies, the ownership of Aquila-BST was acquired by Systems Development Corporation (SDC) in California. Berthiaume was invited to become president of Aquila-BST operations and accepted. In the late 1970s, he purchased the company back from SDC, and Aquila-BST reverted to Canadian ownership becoming Le Groupe BST.

Computel Systems: beginning a new era

However, the quantum jump in Canadian service operations did not occur until late 1967, with the formation of Computel Systems Ltd., Ottawa, the first computer utility to issue shares as a public company.

By this time, increasingly sophisticated facilities were about to add a new dimension to the services scene. In the fifties and early sixties, data processing services had been provided in batch, over the counter mode. Users brought their data to the computer site, where the data was processed and then returned "over the counter." By the mid-sixties, however, the transmission of data over telephone wires or by microwave circuitry had become technologically possible. The computer-communications merge had begun.

Computel—"Computing capacity by telephone"—was the first company to take advantage of these new remote communications capabilities. The company was founded by two young entrepreneurs, Warren Beamish, 30, and Robert Horwood, 28. Dark-haired, clean cut Mr. Beamish, who is described by a colleague as "a restless, dynamic powerhouse of a man," was manager of large scale marketing for the Univac Division of Sperry Rand. Mr. Horwood, "the man with the beard," was, according to the same source, "a more polished diamond— keenly intelligent with a wide range of interests, articulate, enthusiastic and energetic, but always willing to listen." He was chief of the computer systems division of the Operations Research group in the National Energy Board.

In 1967, the two joined forces. Their original plan was to form a private company, secure financial backing to lease a Univac 1108 processor, and provide computer power to clients either over the counter or through telephone linked communications facilities. Computel would function as a utility, an alternative for the customer to ownership of his own computer.

"At the time we started up, everyone told us we were crazy," Mr. Horwood says. "People in Canada didn't believe that remote access computing would work."

Nevertheless, fired with purpose, Beamish and Horwood prepared to launch their venture. By the fall of 1967, Computel Systems Ltd. was a legal entity, and a number of potential clients had been lined up, including the federal government. The Treasury Board had assured the two young men that whenever possible, the government would purchase computer time from private resources. However, they faced an unanticipated series of obstacles.

In early October, Univac informed them that they could not lease an 1108. They were told that the company's United States principals considered the new company's credit rating too weak for a leasing arrangement. Computel could buy an 1108—for more than $2 million cash—but leasing was out. The machine would be held for them until October 31, less than three weeks away.

With introductions from investment firm A.E. Ames and Company Limited, Mr. Beamish and Mr. Horwood rushed to New York City seeking funds. The only offer was from National Computer Leasing, a subsidiary of American Export Lines. They agreed to finance the company, but with the stipulation that the stock would be owned by the American company with Beamish and Horwood acting as employee-managers. "We didn't like that idea too much and decided to look elsewhere," Warren Beamish says.

A.E. Ames then contacted some Canadian financial institutions, who indicated interest—provided that $1 million U.S. money could be raised. Further frantic efforts to obtain funds were somewhat more successful and Canadian interest began to strengthen. On October 30, 1967, one day before the Univac deadline, potential investors met at Toronto in the board room of A.E. Ames. From 9 a.m. to 2 p.m., Mr. Beamish and Mr. Horwood presented their case. Then they awaited the verdict.

"All afternoon we sat on tenterhooks," Mr. Beamish says. "At 5 p.m., the first bid came in from Guardian Growth Fund, Ltd. Fifteen minutes later, the whole issue was sold out. A few minutes after that, people were calling, asking to get in on the issue. $2.5 million had been committed."

However, the company's immediate need was for $200,000 cash for the down payment to guarantee delivery of the 1108. Another obstacle arose. Computel was still a private company and could not actually sell stock. Conversion to a public company would take at least three weeks, and Computel needed the money the next day.

The president of A.E. Ames called the president of Univac to explain the situation. "No problem, no problem at all," was the response. "I always knew the boys would get their money. Go ahead."

Go ahead "the boys" did. But not without one last obstacle. The Ottawa computing centre was scheduled to open for business in January 1968. On a cold December 24, 1967, the 1108 was delivered. Mr. Horwood was watching intently as the crane operator prepared to transfer the computer from the moving van to Computel's office on Laurier Avenue.

"One of the fellows in the moving van started to really put his shoulder to the central processing unit, and I yelled at him, 'Hey, be careful with that. It's worth half a million bucks.'

"The crane operator heard me and said, 'How much did you say that was?' And I repeated, 'About half a million bucks.'

"'Well I'm not lifting that,' he said. 'I'm only insured for $40,000'."

Bob Horwood stood helplessly by as the operator unhooked his gear, put his crane away and left. It was Christmas Eve—nothing could be done to increase the insurance until after the holiday. The 1108 was pushed back onto the moving van to await installation on December 27.

However, Computel operations began on schedule on January 15, 1968, with Warren Beamish as president and Bob Horwood as vice president.

"From the beginning we knew we had to be cash positive—we had to do $50,000 worth of business for the month of February," Mr. Beamish says. "We also had to have six remote batch processors operating and communicating to the 1108. Bay Street was watching carefully, and computer experts were betting we'd go bankrupt.

"By January 15, 1968, we had three terminals operating online.

By February 1, we had five terminals. In the first three weeks we had done $8,000 worth of business. By the end of February, we had sent out invoices for $54,000 and by March 1 had collected $50,000."

An auspicious beginning for the precedent-setting company. By its third quarter, Computel was running at a profit and was ready to consider expansion. In January a second service centre, also equipped with a Univac 1108 began operations in Toronto, and shortly afterward an IBM 360/65 was installed in additional Ottawa facilities.

"The Dominion Bureau of Statistics (now Statistics Canada) needed extra IBM 360/65 time and had said that if we could provide that capability, we could have the contract," Mr. Beamish says. "I had always felt that a service bureau should be like a hydro utility—it should have large machines from Univac, IBM, Control Data, and others, to provide cycles to anybody, no matter what type of machine he had at the other end. I had plans to put in another large machine (from various manufacturers) each month from then on."

Over the counter trading in Computel shares began in February 1968. The price went from a low of $100 in March to a high of $270 in May. In that month, the stock was split 10 to one, converting to $27 a share, and went to a further high of $35 in September. In February, 1969, the stock was listed on the Toronto Stock Exchange, reaching a high of $50 per share that year.

"We were looked on as wonder kids," Mr. Beamish says. "No service business in Canada had ever raised a cent through public money. Now every brokerage house in the country was trying to find a computer company they could sponsor and bring public."

As a result, the marketplace was flooded with companies offering computer services. Between December, 1968, and June, 1969, more than 20 new service organizations began competing for business. Eventually, many of these failed. Those that did not, struggled hard for survival.

Computel was one of the survivors. However, in the fall of 1969, the "wonder kids" parted ways. Warren Beamish resigned as president of Computel, later severing completely his connections with the company to work for University Computing Company International Inc. (UCC) of Dallas, Texas. "I still hoped eventually to get Computel back," he says 13 years later.

In December, Bob Horwood was named president.

It was a difficult period for the new company. Computel had three computer centres to maintain, and federal government spending on computer time had been sharply reduced. Competition was heated. Nevertheless, Computel resisted a take-over offer made by UCC, and rallied forces to prepare for further challenges in the seventies.

Systems Dimensions Limited

The federal government was Canada's largest single user of computer power. Therefore it is not surprising that a second computer service company would be formed to compete in Ottawa with Computel for government business.

Systems Dimensions Limited (SDL) was incorporated in March 1968 by three IBM graduates from the Ottawa office: George Fierheller, Guy Morton, and John D. Russell. Mr. Fierheller, SDL's first and only president, states firmly, "We did not leave IBM with any idea of starting a computer services organization. We wanted the flexibility of being on our own and not part of a huge organization."

The catalyzing opportunity was a federal government project to computerize the physical resources of Canada. Under a fixed price contract, IBM was participating in the Canada Land Inventory Project, known as ARDA (Agricultural Rehabilitation and Development Agency). By the fall of 1967, the project was well along and well over budget.

Mr. Fierheller, Mr. Morton, and Mr. Russell, who were working on ARDA, decided a concentrated effort for about a year was needed, and that they were the right people to do this for the government.

"The whole plot was hatched in the Colonel By Lounge in the Chateau Laurier one evening in late January, 1968," George Fierheller says. "John, Guy and I decided we would leave IBM, form a small consulting firm, and offer our services to the government to complete the ARDA project. We reasoned correctly that IBM would be delighted to be rid of the cash drain, and the government would be equally pleased to get the project completed quickly."

The three submitted their resignations to IBM president Bill Moore, who later was to be associated with SDL as chairman of the company's Executive Committee.

"As there was no immediate thought of expanding beyond the original trio, we decided we might as well have whatever titles appealed," Mr. Fierheller continues. "I became president and John and Guy each became vice presidents of a firm with no employees. This gave us a sense of power."

The plan was for Guy Morton and George Fierheller to spend most of their time on the ARDA project, while John Russell also looked around for new clients.

However, within four months, the group that did not want to be part of a "huge corporation" was launched on a course that would eventually turn SDL into one of the largest service organizations in Canada.

The original impetus came from an Ottawa lawyer and chartered accountant, Redmond Quain, Jr., who had been observing Computel's operations and believed that a business opportunity existed for a large company to provide a similar type of computing services. He advised SDL to go public, predicting that the financial community would support a multi-million dollar underwriting.

"Red's ideas fell on fertile ground," Mr. Fierheller says. "John, Guy and I had always felt that Computel had slightly missed the market. Ottawa was an IBM town in those days. It seemed to us that the conversion of accounts from in-house computers to a large IBM remote job entry facility was a natural. We knew the equipment and knew exactly how to go about launching such a program."

George Fierheller is a trim, lean man, with a disarming smile, a responsible, to-the-point manner, and sound grasp of business principles as well as of computer technology. His plan for the new service facility included construction of a completely new type of building that would be oriented toward the new computer industry, acquisition of the largest and fastest commercially available mainframe (the newly announced IBM 360/85), and a new approach to charging for the use of computer time.

"When George Fierheller put SDL together, he created a benchmark in the service industry," a colleague comments. "He developed software so that he could account for the computer cycles a client used, and bill the client for those cycles and the equipment used in each application that was run. It was the first time that a billing system could break a processing job into small units, so that the customer could be charged according to those units."

To operate the new business, Mr. Fierheller and his colleagues recruited "the right people to do the job." Among them were Frank Van Humbeck, who had left IBM to work for Domtar in Montreal, as well as Don Pounder, Brian Greenleaf, Charlie Ploeg and others from the Ottawa IBM office. Jack Kyle, IBM Toronto branch manager, became general manager of SDL and recommended Bill Beairsto as director of marketing. University of Waterloo Professor Wesley Graham became a member of the board of directors.

Mr. Quain's predictions proved to be sound. SDL was underwritten for $17.5 million by Wood Gundy. Bridge financing had been provided by the Toronto Dominion Bank. In February, 1969, the company went public. The stock was substantially oversubscribed, doubled in price the first day it was offered, and increased another 25 per cent by the second day.

In June, 1969, the SDL Systemcentre opened its doors. Almost immediately, the government announced the postponement of the ARDA contract award. SDL had expected that revenues from that contract would carry the new company while a client base was being built. An alternate plan had to be found quickly.

It was found through an arrangement with AGT Data Systems Limited, then headed by Gerry Wanless and Ted White. With offices in Toronto and Montreal, AGT agreed to market SDL services to commercial enterprises in the two cities. Gary Hughes in Toronto and Dave Carlisle in Montreal would handle the operations that would enable SDL to expand its client base in the two largest non-government areas in the country, and would free them from exclusive dependence on government business.

By the end of the sixties, a base of commercial clients was building up and SDL looked hopefully to the future.

Dataline Systems Limited

One of Computel's first customers was National Computing Services, a Toronto consulting firm headed by John Galipeau and Dr. Joseph Paradi. Like most of Computel's users, they were technically oriented. John Galipeau was an electrical engineer. Joe Paradi had a Ph.D. in chemical engineering.

However, Dr. Paradi believed there was a market for services that went one step further than those offered by Computel. He envisioned a service company that would provide an interactive environment, where a customer would have a typewriter-like terminal on which a program could be entered, debugged, and compiled before being submitted to the central computer.

Similar services were being offered by General Electric and by IBM, but were limited in the amount of computing and core facilities available. Online storage was also extremely expensive.

"So we said, 'If we want this type of service and can't buy it, what would it take to make it?'," Dr. Paradi says.

Joe Paradi is a dynamo. His dark eyes sparkle, his bald head gleams, he speaks quickly, expressing his ideas with passion and conviction. He gives the impression of a man whose mind is always alert, questioning, assessing possibilities.

Certainly these were the qualities he displayed in exploring the technical possibilities for the facilities the new company would required.

After several months of intensive investigations, a Digital Equipment Corporation DECsystem 10 (then called a PDP-10) was selected as the system that would provide the required hardware and technical facilities for fast turnaround timesharing operations.

Dataline Systems Limited was founded as a private company in August 1968 and started operations in January 1969. "We put together a business plan to provide clients with a teletypewriter and the freedom to use as much core, as big a portion of a powerful machine as they needed. We assembled bright staff, contacted prospective clients, and then began looking for financial backing," Dr. Paradi says.

In March, 1969, the $4.7 million Galipeau and Paradi required for the new company was underwritten by Dominion Securities Corporation. Dataline Systems Limited was in business as a public company, with Mr. Galipeau as president and Dr. Paradi as vice president. In 1970, the former withdrew from Dataline, and Joe Paradi became president.

In the early years, Dataline provided interactive timesharing computer services to users who were "computer oriented," who wrote and compiled their own programs. The company successfully weathered the rough years of 1969 and 1970 when computer stocks dropped sharply on the market and when many other service companies suffered irreversible losses.

Sales continued to grow, however, and in the early seventies, Dataline would begin to carve its own particular niche in the services industry.

Multiple Access Computer Group

Multiple Access General Computer Corporation was started in 1969 by Robert Parker and Peter Buckley who had met while working for the research division of Northern Electric Ltd. (now Bell Northern Research Inc.). They had been using Control Data computer equipment at Northern Electric and decided to start a service operation based on that equipment. In spite of that fact, they managed to attract two IBM Ottawa employees, Ray Hession and Jay Kurtz to the new company.

Multiple Access went public in 1969 and raised a tremendous amount of backing money. However, Mr. Parker was unable to accomplish his objectives and the company failed financially. Cemp Investments (part of the Bronfman family holdings) assumed control of the company and appointed John McCutcheon, an executive vice president of Cemp, as president of Multiple Access. He was expected to turn the company around and make it the "largest service bureau in Canada."

Its game plan was to offer the widest range of software and data processing services possible—to be a computing service firm, a software house, and a hardware supplier (an OEM selling equipment manufactured by other hardware companies)—in short, a panacea for the Canadian computer user.

To reach those ends, Multiple Access began acquiring other similar firms early in the seventies. A great deal of activity lay ahead for the company as the new decade began.

The race was on

Companies like Polycom Systems Limited, formed in 1968 in Toronto by J. Philip Humfrey, were unfortunate victims of the rising tide of investment speculation that marked the turn of the decade. The company showed a profit in its first year, then got caught in the recession with machine capability well beyond the customer demand. Its venture capital controlling shareholders appointed Allan Ormsby as president of the floundering company in 1972. He then changed the hardware configuration, created a timesharing service, and turned the company around.

Consolidated Computer Inc. was also started in the 1967 period in Kingston as a timesharing service, as has been noted in an earlier chapter.

Comshare Limited began in 1968 as a small service operation under the name Ontario Time Sharing Services Limited. It offered online computer power to the scientific and engineering community in southern Ontario. An affiliation with the U.S. firm Comshare Inc. and financial backing from Polymer Corporation Limited, the Sarnia, Ontario, based crown corporation, were already in place when Englishman Derek Price and six associates arrived on the scene. Price became the Canadian president and his associates returned to England to set up Comshare U.K. The product offerings were changed in 1971 to provide more specialized, customer-oriented packages in the financial, data base, and graphics fields. This successful firm has branches throughout southern Ontario as well as in Vancouver, Calgary, and Montreal.

Alphatext Limited was started in Ottawa in 1969 by Glenn McInnes, Peter Fedirchuk, and John Bobak, all IBM graduates, as a supplier of word processing and printing services. McInnes, then 26 years old, had tried to interest IBM in a project to fit together text editing, phototypesetting and information retrieval in a single package. When the suggestion fell on deaf ears, he raised about $1 million through family friends to start a firm to do it himself. In June 1977, Shell Canada Ltd. acquired a controlling interest in the company. This infusion of capital enabled Alphatext Ltd. to continue software development and to tap into new markets.

Around the same time, two more IBM employees, Jack Davies and Tony Thurston, started a company called Softwarehouse Ltd., which later became part of Systems Dimensions Limited and still later was reincarnated as Systemhouse Ltd.

Comcheq Services Ltd. was one of the first computing services firms in the City of Winnipeg and perhaps the first to specialize in payroll applications. The company was formed in 1968 by William Loewen, who had been comptroller with Ideal Brass and Plating. He set up an affiliation with Fidelity Trust in Manitoba in 1973 and expanded his company into other provinces. The company now has branches in seven cities across the country.

Also in Winnipeg in 1968, Symbionics opened its doors to provide general data processing services. The company declared bankruptcy in 1970 and was taken over by the provincial government and renamed Phoenix Data Ltd. It was later called Cybershare and sold to a group of local data processing specialists headed by John Turner, Les Foden, Don Turner and Art Balageer.

Geodigit, a seismic and geophysical data processing firm, began in Calgary in 1968 with Control Data Equipment. The firm is the North American operation of a French geophysical contracting organization, Compagnie General de Geophysique.

Newfoundland and Labrador Computer Services Ltd., formed in 1969 in St. John's, Newfoundland, with Harold Miller as president, was the first provincially-owned data processing service firm in Canada. Although not a crown corporation, its shares were owned by ministers in the Newfoundland provincial government. Although its first customers—and the thrust behind its creation—were the Province of Newfoundland, Memorial University of Newfoundland, and Newfoundland Hydro, the list has grown to include other government departments and some commercial clients.

The above firms represent the type of data processing services companies that were started during the halcyon days of the late sixties, although the list is by no means complete.

In late 1969, the bloom began to fade from the flower that had been the darling of the stock market. Suddenly, it was no longer in vogue to be a computer company offering shares on the open market, although business continued to grow and applications expanded. Some of the smaller companies fell by the wayside. Others were merged into consortiums with similar small firms. And as can be seen, many have continued to exist and survive, providing specialized and localized data processing services to an ever-present small business user community.

Shows and publications

By the end of the 1960s, the data processing field was so well established in Canada that it warranted the addition of specially dedicated trade publications and exhibitions.

In 1968, Maclean-Hunter Ltd. of Toronto brought out the first edition of *Canadian Datasystems* magazine. Other publications were to follow to service the expanding data processing market. Both the Data Processing Management Association and the Canadian Information Processing Society produced magazines strictly for their own memberships.

There was an abortive attempt at a new computer publication by Southam Communications Ltd. in the early 1970s. And still later, in the mid-seventies, Whitsed Publishing Ltd. of Toronto introduced its *ComputerData* magazine and Plessman Publications of Montreal (now of Toronto) began publishing its *Computing Canada* data processing newspaper.

In 1969, Maclean-Hunter's trade show division announced the first annual Canadian Computer Show. The industry also had the Canadian Business Equipment Show, as well as the association (DPMA, CIPS) exhibitions, as vehicles to exhibit the still-new computer technology.

Since that time, many exhibitions have grown up around the industry to promote new computer products and to specialize in new areas of technology such as office automation, data communications, or individual market applications.

In the area of shows and exhibitions, Canada's world fair in 1967, Expo '67, rates mention. Canadian General Electric had contracted with Expo Corporation to install one of its CGE 625 computers to run the Expo site, handling admissions, ticket sales, lodging requirements, and reservations for visitors to the fair (LogExpo). The computer site on the fairgrounds became one of the exhibits as well.

IBM Canada was asked to install a computer in the Canadian

pavilion with space in two theme pavilions (Man the Producer, and Man and the Community). The exhibit utilized an IBM 360 Model 50 (manufactured in the U.S.—the Canadian-made 360/40 was not powerful enough to handle everything that IBM wanted it to do). Dick Taylor was in charge of the project and calls it "possibly the most complex computer installation in Canada at the time."

The computer system was used to handle reservations for tickets to the various theatre shows taking place in the pavilions ("the 1967 equivalent to the BASS ticket agency," says Mr. Taylor). The application died "from too much success," according to Mr. Taylor, because people began lining up at the information kiosks for theatre tickets instead of at the pavilions themselves, and often found that the tickets they wanted had all been sold for that day. As well, because of the demand for tickets, the kiosk personnel were not able to dispense the information they had been set up to provide. The application, ReservExpo, caused some frustrations. "One unhappy visitor punched a kiosk hostess in the face one afternoon in June," says Mr. Taylor, "and that was the end of ReservExpo."

Two IBM 360/30 computers were also used to run the Expo display boards throughout the grounds. "The only place we could put them was in the CGE pavilion, a rather ticklish situation," says Mr. Taylor. "They ended up under the walkway that went through the middle of the pavilion, in an effort to hide them. But their red exteriors made them very conspicuous nevertheless.

"The exhibition was good for us and for Canadian General Electric," Taylor comments. "It was a great test of the systems' capabilities (the ReservExpo terminals, located in the open-air kiosks, had to work under all weather conditions—in the blazing summer sun, wind, rain, dust, etc.). And the exposure to public attention and opinion was better than any advertisement."

After the world's fair closed down, the CGE 625 was installed at Celanese Corporation in Montreal.

In retrospect

"It was an interesting time, because computers were just beginning to be associated in a practical way with communications," says Dick Taylor. "Throughout the decade, large organizations were becoming interested in that capability. We were fortunate to have the opportunity to demonstrate to the world at large what computers could actually do, at places like Expo and the new computer shows."

A core of technology had been developed for such future spin-off enterprises as data communications and office automation.

Robert Johnson *(left)*, Josef Kates and Leonard Casciato with UTEC, the massive, room-size computer developed at the University of Toronto in the early 1950s.

Bill Wade *(left)*, John Aitchison and Dr. Kelly Gotlieb in the University of Toronto Computation Centre, May 24, 1960.

Hudson Stowe *(right)*, Comptroller for Manufacturers Life Insurance Company, and two of the company's employees work on the new system, installed in March 1956.

Dr. Kelly Gotlieb *(left)*, and representatives from Canadian National Railways observe Audrey Bates transmit data from the University of Toronto Ferut to the University of Saskatchewan during the late 1950s.

Kenneth Iverson, the creator of APL explaining the finer points of the language.

(Above) Confederation Life data centre circa 1958, with IBM 705 computer.

(Upper right) Air Canada (then Trans-Canada Airlines) employee inserts computer card into terminal of Ferranti-Packard's Gemini computer reservation system, 1961.

(Lower right) Hostesses at 14 information booths strategically located around Expo 67 helped make visits more enjoyable by providing reservations to the 22 pavilion theatres, in one of the first applications by IBM computers at a world's fair.

The simple truth about Data Processing

To get the on-time information they require, many executives visualize the need for a battery of expensive equipment. Yet there is a low-cost system that fits your company as it stands and as it grows.

I'm the girl you married. Remember?

1959

1960

"Any size business can afford this EDP system!"

1963

DATA ENTRY AND VALIDATION COSTS CAN EAT UP THE LARGEST CHUNK OF YOUR EDP BUDGET

1969

1970

1973

Advertisements for computer manufacturers reflected state of the art in marketing as well as in computers.

George Fierheller *(left)*, R.G. Taylor and Michael Burns sign
agreement merging Systems Dimensions Limited with Datacrown.

PART THREE

The Seventies and Beyond

The Industry Matures

*T*HROUGHOUT THE SEVENTIES, the computer became not only a dynamic tool indispensable to business, education, government and industry, but also a household word. True, there were still high priests of technology speaking in arcane tongues and performing mysterious high-tech rites. However, the apprehension initially felt by many at the dawning of the information age had evolved to an appreciation of computer capability and confidence in users' ability to put the new technology to work.

As computer communications became a practical reality, the number of applications skyrocketed, and Canada began to take its part in the Wired World.

1

Communications: Canada takes a leading role

*B*Y THE END of the 1960s, the transmission of computer data over regular voice telephone lines had become accepted as a convenient method of sending information between two locations for batch processing and retrieval. To conform to the specifications of the voice lines, computer signals had to be converted from digital to analog, then back to digital at the receiving end. Over long distances, the signal had to be regenerated at every switching stage. But noises on the lines were also regenerated, causing some problems with the reception.

These forays into data transmission in the late 1960s were not the first attempts to send data between two points in Canada. As described in Part One of this book, a data project in 1955 involved the Universities of Toronto and Saskatchewan, teleprinter terminals at either end, the use of Canadian National Railway telegraph lines and the very powerful (for its time) Ferut computer at the University of Toronto.

The following year, in 1956, Canadian National Telecommunications and Canadian Pacific Telecommunications joined forces to introduce Telex (customer-dialed teleprinters) service to North America.

By 1958, the TransCanada Telephone System (TCTS) had built a cross-country microwave network over which black and white television signals (for both the CBC and CTV networks), telephone, telegraph, network radio, data and TWX signals could be carried simultaneously. In 1962, CN/CP (Canadian National/

Canadian Pacific) Telecommunications announced that it was going to build its own microwave system from Montreal to Vancouver. Approval was received from the Department of Transport and the system was completed in 1964.

The rivalry between these two communications giants has contributed to the fact that Canada has not just one, but two of the best data communications networks in the world.

The gathering momentum in various areas of the data processing and data communications field caused the federal government to take a harder look at the new and growing industry.

Many in the industry believe that the spur to increased government attention was the purchase by CN/CP Telecommunications of a 50 per cent interest in Computer Sciences Canada Ltd., the Canadian subsidiary of a large U.S. computer services organization. When the government approved the purchase, a number of service companies formed an *ad hoc* group in 1969 to prepare a brief voicing their protest. Their fear was that if the common carriers went into the computer service business, the carriers might offer clients preferential rates on their communication facilities, while charging regular rates to their competitors.

The government refused to reverse its approval and CN and CP retained their involvement in Computer Sciences for many years. However, government interest in this new segment of Canadian business had been intensified.

By 1970, users, suppliers, researchers and the government began to realize that there was little known about the field of data communications. The Science Council of Canada set up a Committee on Computers and Communications to do a study on computer applications and technology. Dr. Leon Katz, chairman of physics at the University of Saskatchewan, was the chairman of the study committee. Dr. Eric Manning, now director of the Computer Communications Network Group at the University of Waterloo, was one of the committee members.

A report titled "A Trans Canada Computer Communications Network: Phase One of a Major Program in Computers" (Science Council of Canada Report No. 13) ensued from the study.

"Through the study, we learned about the early work that was being done on packet switching in England and the United States," says Dr. Manning. "We also learned about the state of things in Canada, and I must admit it was very discouraging. We had managed to convince ourselves that data communications networks were going to become the new nerve system for the organizations of the nation.

"Our report may have been somewhat alarmist to some readers. We said essentially that the TransCanada Telephone System should create a first-rate data communications service. We had in mind something like the ARPA network in the United States, only on a commercial basis. Or, if TCTS weren't prepared to do it, then the government should do it for them. We felt this was too important to be allowed to fall through the cracks."

Also in 1970, a group of experts worked as a Telecommission under the federal Department of Communications (DOC) to study the field of telecommunications in Canada. Their report, *Instant World*, was published in 1971. The work of the Telecommission was continued by the Canadian Computer/Communications Task Force, established by the federal cabinet, under the auspices of DOC. The group, headed by Dr. H.J. von Baeyer, former president of Acres Intertel Ltd., was requested to "develop and recommend specific policies and institutions that would ensure the orderly, rational and efficient growth of combined computer/communications systems in the public interest."

The Task Force spent more than 18 months studying the presentations made by representatives of government, industry, business and public institutions. Their two-volume report, *Branching Out*, was published in 1972. It contained 39 recommendations and emphasized "the general pervasiveness, both actual and projected, of computer/communications throughout the Canadian social fabric and consequent necessity for governments at all levels to recognize computer/communications as a key area of social and industrial activity."

It noted that "Canadian expertise is second to none in high technology areas. The major Canadian failing lies in our inability to fully exploit opportunities and insufficient clarity in the definition of objectives. There appears to be a delay in the acceptance of Canadian technological developments until they have been acknowledged by other countries."

The Task Force urged federal and provincial governments to

take steps to strengthen the Canadian computer/ communications industry and to "co-ordinate its development to the benefit of Canadian society."

One of the recommendations in the report was the creation of a computer/communications Focal Point for strategic planning and program co-ordination. Subsequently, the Treasury Board Secretariat was established to oversee the management of data processing within the government, and the Computer/ Communications Secretariat was formed with DOC to improve the interface between business and government. In March, 1978, the latter was disbanded as an economic measure.

"With *Branching Out*, Canada was ahead of its time both in recognizing the marriage of computers and communications, and in articulating a global policy concerning informatics, at a time when the governments of other nations did not think about it at all," comments Gaston Beauséjour. "Canada was the first country to see the computer industry as a social phenomenon worthy of policy."

However, M. Beauséjour believes that *Branching Out* was "a brilliant articulation that failed" because it did not attract the attention of businessmen and politicians "who are the decision-makers, who make things go."

He says: "The report did not produce the positive results that might have occurred in the economy if it had made these decision-makers aware of the potential consequences of techno-logical development that this nation was the first to identify and highlight."

At the same time, TCTS undertook two market research studies to look at the needs of users. They learned that data was indeed a separate business from voice communications. In 1970, the Computer Communications Region (CCR) was formed to focus on data. That group became the Computer Communications/Network Services, which brought together computer communications planning with long distance plan-ning. Eventually in 1972, the name was changed to the Computer Communications Group.

That same year (1972), communications in Canada got a boost when the country's—and the world's—first commercial domes-tic geostationary communications satellite, Telesat Canada's

Anik A-I, was launched from Cape Canaveral in Florida. The satellite began receiving and transmitting voice, data and television signals to earth stations situated across Canada by January, 1973. Telesat Canada, incorporated in 1969, is a private commercial venture jointly owned by the Canadian Telecommunications Common Carriers (the major telephone companies and CN/CP Telecommunications) and the federal government.

In 1973 as well, both the TransCanada Telephone System (TCTS) and CN/CP Telecommunications established their respective cross-Canada private digital data communications networks. Dataroute from TCTS and Infoexchange from CN/CP offered dedicated circuit switching between set points *via* their respective cross-country microwave networks. Dataroute is said to be the longest digital data network in the world (although West Germany's is expected to be equal in length when it is completed).

In order to use the facilities of either Dataroute or Infoexchange, users had to be subscribers of the particular network they wished to access. Dedicated circuit switching provided a much better method of sending data than regular voice lines had, but because the lines were dedicated to one user site per line, a great deal of data had to be sent over the lines to make them cost effective. The user paid for the line even when it was not being used.

"We realized that because Dataroute was a private line with dedicated facilities, it was poor utilization of the facilities," says Andrew M. McMahon, vice president of engineering for Bell Canada and a former director of the Computer Communications Group. "But it was inexpensive in comparison with sending data over standard voice lines. CCG felt there could be better utilization of existing facilities and wanted to look at a shared approach on the public network through something called packet switching. There had been some work done on packet switching on the ARPA network, but that was military rather than commercial. And Larry Roberts was just starting a packet switched network called Telenet in the United States.

"The basic Dataroute technology had come from Tran Communications of California," Mr. McMahon explains. "We asked

Tran to set up a Canadian operation to produce units and to do some work on packet switching. Northern Telecom Limited and Bell-Northern Research created a 'packet switcher,' the SL/10, which would break the data into packets of a certain length to be sent across our digital network. We were the first telephone company in the world to use such a system."

Subscribers' data could now be made into packets, each with an address, and sent simultaneously across the lines. This would allow the lines to be "public," used by a wide variety of subscribers, thus keeping the cost per subscriber to a minimum.

"The service bureaus were the driving force in telecommunications," says Mr. McMahon. "They demanded high speed communications, faster connect times, accuracy. They've now been surpassed by the banks and other large corporations, many of whom have their own private networks and also use the public data networks."

TCTS started work on its packet switched network in 1974 and demonstrated it in 1976. The University of Waterloo and the University of Alberta were among the first trial customers of Datapac, as the network was called.

Also in 1976, CN/CP Telecommunications announced its own packet switched network, Infoswitch. Both CN/CP and TCTS public packet switched networks piggybacked their existing circuit switched networks and also used the Anik satellites.

By the time these networks were announced, the Anik A-II satellite (launched April 20, 1973) and the Anik A-III satellite (launched May 7, 1975) were in geostationary orbit above the equator.

Each satellite's life is about five to seven years, at which time the fuel and batteries are no longer useful, and the satellite is pulled out of orbit and into deeper space. Its "parking space" is then available for another satellite. The Anik B satellite was launched on December 15, 1978 and occupied the parking space vacated by Anik A-II. The first of three powerful Anik C satellites and the first of two 24-channel Anik D satellites will have been launched before the end of 1982.

The satellites have not only improved voice, data communications and television capabilities, but have also allowed national newspapers like the Toronto-based *Globe and Mail* to produce a satellite edition beamed to centres such as Vancouver, Calgary and London (England) for printing and distribution.

Both voice and data communications to other countries are handled through Teleglobe Canada (formerly the Canadian Overseas Telecommunications Corporation) *via* satellite and underseas cable.

Communications products: Canadian innovation to the rescue

With the advent of data communications capabilities, users could place computer terminals or minicomputers in remote locations and communicate back to the central computer. The concept of distributed data processing (DDP) pervaded all aspects of the user community. Smaller computers could feed a number of local terminals for immediate processing of local data, then the information could be transmitted to other regional computers and to the head office computer as well, when needed.

But this application brought with it the need for specialized data communications equipment that would allow the user to connect the various terminals and computers in each location to one another and to the common carrier networks.

High speed modems (modulator/demodulators) were available for long haul connections, but for short haul internal communications, a product called a limited distance data set was needed. Two Canadian companies entered the market about the same time with this type of product and have competed domestically and abroad quite effectively.

Develcon Electronics Ltd. started in 1969 in Saskatoon as a partnership when two engineering professors at the University of Saskatchewan, George Spark and Jerry Huff, developed a short haul data set for use with the computers on the U of S campus. By 1974, the company was producing its LDDS (limited distance data set) in volume and marketing it to the four western telephone companies. The product was later adopted by those telephone companies as a standard offering. At this point, Nigel

Hill (who became president of the company in 1978) came on board as vice president of marketing.

In the summer of 1978, Develcon introduced a modular intelligent front end switching system, Dataswitch, that performs much the same function in a data communications network as the central switching office does in a modern telephone network. The first of these intelligent switches was installed at the University of Saskatchewan in 1978. The following year, the first "offshore" Dataswitch was installed at the Virginia Polytechnical Institute and State University in the United States.

A U.S. subsidiary of Develcon was established in Doylestown, Pennsylvania in 1979, making Develcon one of Canada's growing number of multinational companies. In the intervening years, the company's products have also been marketed in Britain, Central Europe, the Middle and Far East through distributors, where the competition from U.S. companies such as Micom and Infotron and another Canadian multinational, Gandalf Technologies Inc., is intense.

Gandalf Technologies Inc. of Ottawa was formed in 1970 as Gandalf Data Communications Ltd. by partners Des Cunningham and Colin Patterson to produce limited distance modems that would transmit digital signals over an analog telephone line. The company received a request from a university for a system to use the modems in conjunction with a private switching arrangement to be installed on two large mainframe computers. This resulted in the development of Gandalf's Private Automatic Computer Exchange (PACX), similar to the telephone PABX.

Gandalf became a multinational in 1976 with the establishment of a U.S. subsidiary in Wheeling, Illinois. The company also opened an office in Britain at the end of the decade to handle European sales.

Develcon and Gandalf have certainly proved that Canadian technology and know-how can be exported and flourish on the international market. They have also paved the way for other Canadian companies to develop and market world class communications technology.

The Saskatoon area, today known locally as "Silicon Flats," has spawned other high technology enterprises besides Develcon.

SED Systems Inc., although not incorporated until 1972,

evolved from the 1956 start-up of the Space Engineering Division (SED) of the University of Saskatchewan. Originally, its activities consisted of the design and construction of rocket payloads for upper atmospheric research being done at the National Research Council.

In 1973, the company developed its first telecommunications product, a telephone autodialer. Today, SED Systems is involved in telecommunications, aerospace and agricultural research and production. There was some involvement in videotex/teletext in the late 1970s, when SED was in the process of developing an information provider terminal. The company abandoned its work in this area to concentrate on other projects. SED became a multinational with the establishment of a subsidiary in Memphis, Tennessee in 1981. Since then, the company has experienced difficulties, reporting a $4 million loss on revenues of $12 million in fiscal 1982.

Northern Telecom Limited moved its entire optical systems division to Saskatoon in late 1981. The Saskatchewan Telecommunications Corporation (Sask Tel) was planning to install a large optical fiber telephone and communications network—a contract that was awarded to Northern Telecom with the proviso that that company open a plant in Saskatchewan to produce the optical fiber required for the project.

The University of Saskatchewan is responsible for the birth of a great deal of the high technology industry in Saskatoon, but that industry's growth has been fostered by the engineering and marketing know-how in its companies.

The city of Saskatoon also boasts a 120-acre research park called Innovation Place. The park is run by the Crown-owned Saskatchewan Economic Development Corporation (SEDCO). As well, there are the Saskatchewan Research Council, the Kelsey Institute of Applied Arts and Science, and a number of smaller high technology firms. Senstek manufactures electronic machinery monitors. AEL Microtel has a telecommunications plant in the city. And Startco develops digital conveyors.

"There are well over 1,000 people working in high technology in Saskatoon," says Nigel Hill of Develcon. "For a city with a population of approximately 160,000, that represents a fair percentage. We're proud of the contribution we make to the industry and feel that the work done in high technology in this province is equal to that done elsewhere in the country."

British Columbia also has a small high technology community, centred around a research area called Discovery Park.

MacDonald, Dettwiler & Associates Ltd. (MDA) was formed by John S. MacDonald and Vern Dettwiler in 1969 to meet the demands for a systems house with complete design and implementation capabilities. According to Denny Doyle, who was then president of Digital Equipment Canada Ltd., MDA was started in John MacDonald's basement as a Digital Equipment OEM (third party supplier).

Today the company is part of the high technology community with its remote sensing and meteorological satellite processing systems.

AEL Microtel is a very visible part of the community, with its telecommunications products and involvement in the videotex/teletext market. The company was started in the late 1970s as a joint venture of GTE Lenkurt and the British Columbia Telephone System (BCTel).

The product range includes state-of-the-art electronic switching and transmission systems and subscriber telephone equipment, as well as Telidon terminals. Much of the research for the company's products is done by a subsidiary, Microtel Pacific Research, whose president, John C. Madden, was formerly with the federal Department of Communications.

Impact Information Systems, one of Canada's leading suppliers of local area networking products, is also a foster child of BCTel. The company's three partners, Roy Pepper, Gerry Sawkins and Horst Neher all worked for the telephone company before deciding to set up their own operation in 1980. They were successful in adapting Canadian communications technology to existing hardware products, creating a local area networking environment for office automation. The company has since expanded into Alberta and Ontario.

"To establish a good high technology community, there has to be a 'leaky bucket' of some sort to provide the native talent and research capability," says Denny Doyle. "In the Ottawa area, it was the National Research Council and Bell-Northern Research as well as the Defence Research Board and the Communications

Research Centre. In other provinces, it has been—and could be in many other cases—the universities and research councils. All the provincial governments would have to do is flood those centres with people and money and create their own 'leaky buckets.' Because of the $10 million per year deficit that we face, I believe there should be a high tech community around every major city in Canada. It is a national necessity."

Ottawa's "Silicon Valley North"

What has happened—and is still happening—in the Ottawa Valley area is still too new to be called history. But it is history in the making.

At the beginning of the 1970s, the Canadian federal government and the computer industry hoped to get in on the semiconductor revolution that had started in California. The countryside surrounding Santa Clara had been dubbed "Silicon Valley" after the silicon-on-sand (SOS) semiconductor chip had been developed there by Intel Corporation. Companies began flocking to the area to begin production of their own high technology devices.

The Canadian government hoped to induce some of this fever in Canada by creating its own "Silicon Valley North" in Ottawa. There was already a great wealth of knowledge in the National Research Council, Bell-Northern Research, the Communications Research Centre, the Defence Research Board, and the city's two universities. Companies such as Computing Devices, Leigh Instruments, Gandalf Technologies, and others had already grown up out of projects or contracts from these "leaky bucket" organizations.

One of the first start-ups was a jointly-funded effort by Northern Telecom and the federal government called Microsystems International. The company had been formed to develop and manufacture semiconductor chips for the Canadian marketplace. However, the venture was not as successful as originally hoped.

Two of the key personalities behind Microsystems—Dr. Mike Cowpland and Terry Matthews—were successful in parlaying the residue talent from Microsystems into Mitel Corporation in 1973. Mitel started producing semiconductors and progressed into digital telephone switching systems. Some of the top engineering and software staff at Mitel were graduates of Consolidated Computer Inc.

Mitel is an interesting phenomenon in that it was the first of a new breed of companies to approach the equity market for funding as the 1970s ended and the 1980s began. What Computel had done a decade earlier, Mitel repeated at that time. Computer stocks had been out of vogue since the early seventies, but with the success of Mitel, another group of high technology firms jumped on the bandwagon. Mitel's progress in product development, product sales, and sales of stock market shares were watched eagerly by the investment community as well as the data processing field.

Gandalf Technologies, Develcon Electronics, Comterm Inc., Cableshare Ltd., Epitek Inc., Northern Telecom, Systemhouse Ltd., Leigh Instruments, Electrohome, and Lumonics are all Canadian companies that offered common shares for sale on the Toronto Stock Exchange in the 1981–82 period. In spite of the poor economic outlook and a depressed stock market, there was still a great deal of interest in high technology stocks.

A synergism developed around Ottawa throughout the 1970s. The federal government's Communications Research Centre (part of the Department of Communications) hit the headlines with the development of the alphageometric Telidon technology. Telidon is the Canadian version of the generic videotex/teletext technology that allows high quality graphics and text to be created from various data bases. It can also turn an ordinary television set into a two-way communications medium with the possibilities of teleshopping, telebanking, plus many other applications.

Telidon has been described as "a solution searching for a problem" by some industry watchers and "one of Canada's best 'better mousetraps' yet" by others. The technology is there, but the main marketplace for it—which was expected to be homes all across the country—hasn't developed as quickly as was expected.

As with a great many Canadian innovations, the interested buyers are mostly "offshore"—in Venezuela, the United States, and one or two other countries. After the first foreign sale was made, the federal government provided some $27.5 million in funds for Canadian firms working in Telidon technology. The high technology industry countered with an influx of $100 million. The federal government later provided an additional $9.5 million to encourage companies to build Telidon products.

One Canadian company in the Ottawa area that has benefited from Telidon is Norpak Ltd. of Pakenham. The company is a family-owned business run by Mark Norton, his brothers John and Christopher, and his sister Maria. (Their father, Joseph Norton, was one of the founders of Computing Devices Company.) Prior to the commencement of production of Telidon information provider terminals, Norpak was already well-known for its color graphics display terminals. The company is doing quite a lot of business in the United States in the Telidon field as well as marketing its display generators. McLaren Power and Paper, a subsidiary of Noranda Mines Limited, invested some $30 million in Norpak in early 1981 in return for a 25 per cent equity share in the company. McLaren also owns 28.5 per cent of Lumonics Inc. (which develops laser devices), and about five per cent of Mitel Corporation.

A newcomer to the high technology field in Ottawa, NABU Manufacturing Corp., opened its doors in early 1981 to manufacture and market microcomputers and home computer terminals that would allow cable television companies to use and exploit videotex.

NABU was the brainchild of John Kelly, formerly one of the founders of Systemhouse Ltd. He took his idea to a few friends who were also in the data processing industry and the resulting amalgamation of Bruce Instruments Ltd. of Almonte (near Ottawa), MFC Microsystems International Ltd. of Ottawa, Computer Innovations Ltd. of Ottawa, Andicom Technical Products of Toronto, Mobius Software Ltd. of Ottawa, and CompuShop Canada Ltd. of Calgary became the new NABU Manufacturing Ltd.

Mr. Kelly enticed Denny Doyle to leave the presidency of Digital Equipment of Canada to take on the presidency of NABU. A number of other people from Ottawa-based hardware, software, consulting, and computing services firms were also sufficiently impressed with the concept to join NABU.

By the middle of 1982, NABU had produced its first cable-compatible computer systems. The company had also purchased

Consolidated Computer Inc. and Volker-Craig Ltd. And it had received a $22.5 million underwriting by Wood Gundy Ltd. and Burns Fry Ltd.

A number of other high technology firms in the Ottawa Valley have benefited from the increased interest focused on the area. Dynalogic Info-Tech Corp. was begun by C. Murray Bell in 1973 to manufacture disk controllers. Over the next decade, the company had begun software development and the production of a business computer system. As well as using OEMs across Canada to market the product, Dynalogic had marketing agreements with distributors in the Netherlands, Sweden, the United Kingdom, Switzerland, Norway, Finland, and the United States. In 1982, design and production of a personal computer compatible with IBM's latest entry had been completed.

Epitek Electronics Ltd. of Kanata was started by president Morley Miller and James Gardner in 1969 to manufacture thick film integrated circuits to be used in communications equipment, data transmission hardware, management information systems, and aerospace instrumentation. The company was acquired in a reverse takeover bid in 1981 by MTS International Services Inc. Because MTS was already a publicly held company with shares trading on the Toronto Stock Exchange, Epitek gained a listing on that exchange.

The computer consulting and software services side of the industry in Ottawa has also received a great deal of attention because of the emphasis placed on the high technology companies. Systemhouse Ltd. and Quasar Ltd. are two of the beneficiaries. More information on both is included in Chapter Three of this section.

Although Bell-Northern Research is headquartered in Ottawa and is considered an integral part of the Silicon Valley North high tech community, it is in reality a national organization.

Bell-Northern Research, one of the Valley's original "leaky buckets," grew out of the Northern Electric research division. Formed in 1971, BNR is a subsidiary of the giant Northern Telecom and Bell Canada organizations. It has become one of the largest individual research and development organizations in Canada with six laboratories in Ottawa and Toronto, Montreal, and Edmonton, as well as labs in California, Michigan, and Minnesota.

The organization is responsible for R&D for the major telephone and telecommunications products manufactured by Northern Telecom. In 1981, the hardware and software divisions of Bell-Northern, which had previously been operated as separated companies, were combined. The software division, Bell-Northern Software Research, Inc. (B-NSR) had been formed in 1976 with John Aitchison, the man who had been IBM Canada's first systems engineer, as president.

Northern Electric, the manufacturing arm of Bell Canada since 1882, was renamed Northern Telecom in 1976. That same year, the outcome of a 10-year federal government study on the vertical integration of the Canadian telecommunications industry was a recommendation that Bell Canada divest itself of Northern Telecom. "Because of its affiliation with Bell Canada, Northern Telecom has 70 per cent of the telecommunications equipment market in Canada," the report stated, objecting to such concentration and lack of competition.

However, Northern Telecom is still 55.2 per cent owned by Bell Canada, although a proposed reorganization could place that ownership under Bell Canada Enterprises. Northern Telecom manufactures both telephone and data communications equipment for Bell and The Computer Communications Group of the TransCanada Telephone System, as well as for outside clients. The company operates internationally with branches, manufacturing plants, and laboratories in the United States, the United Kingdom, Turkey, Switzerland, and Singapore. Canadian facilities are located in Toronto, Ottawa, Calgary, and Saskatoon.

In 1978, Northern Telecom purchased Data 100 Corporation and Sycor Inc., both U.S.-owned minicomputer manufacturers, to form the Electronic Office Systems division. The 1978 NTL annual report stated: "Our interest in these companies is not solely the development of a significant position in the data distribution industry. They are an essential element in the creation of a corporation that will be a leader in the clearly identified trend of a coming together of the telecommunications and data processing technologies. The combined technologies will be the telecommunications industry of the 1980s and beyond ... We believe the future of the telecommunications industry will fall to those companies that can provide total communications network planning and production."

The Electronic Offices Systems division became Northern Telecom Systems Ltd. There were problems in the integration of the Sycor and Data 100 companies into one operating unit. During the 1980 operating year, Northern Telecom Ltd. declared writeoffs and provisions of some $220 million related to the "amount of goodwill and acquired value of the technology investment" in Sycor and Data 100. That year, NTL had a net loss of $185.2 million (including a $163.8 million extraordinary item loss attributed to NTSL). The remaining $56 million NTSL loss was recorded as operating expenses.

In spite of this setback, Northern Telecom is regarded as Canada's most successful high technology corporation. As previously mentioned, the company is involved in manufacturing telephone and telecommunications switching products, optical fiber products, digital switching and transmission systems, LSI (large scale integrated) circuits, as well as products such as the Displayphone voice/data integration terminal.

In the area of optical fibers, another Canadian company—Canstar Communications, a division of Canada Wire and Cable—has gained recognition as a designer and manufacturer of fiber optic couplers, lightguide (fiber optic) cable and cord, and optical line terminating equipment. Formed in 1976 in Toronto, the company's major manufacturing division is in Winnipeg. Through research being done at the University of Toronto, Canstar has become involved in passive local area data network activities.

Networking through X.25 compatible equipment gave rise to another group of Canadian companies. Daedalus Micro-Electronics Limited, formed in 1975 by Richard J. Clarke and Jan Haarink and disbanded in 1980, and ENA Datasystems Inc., started by Dr. Edmunde Newhall, were two Toronto companies producing X.25 switching equipment during the seventies. Memotec Corp. of Montreal produced similar equipment for the Canadian communications marketplace.

ESE Limited, as mentioned in Part Two, was formed in 1964 with the closing of the computer division of Ferranti-Packard. In 1978 ESE was purchased by Codex Corporation, a U.S. manufacturer of communications equipment. Four years later, it became part of the Motorola Information Systems Group. These affiliations have enabled ESE to become one of the country's leading data communications equipment manufacturers and suppliers.

Office automation becomes a byword

The communications thrust and the proliferation of minicomputers and small business computers across the country led to what was soon termed the "office automation revolution."

Office automation encompasses the repetitive office clerical tasks of typing, filing, message delivery—whether by telephone or letter/memo—text manipulation, and other such functions. As computer technology became more sophisticated, it was realized that these functions, and others, could be automated to facilitate their execution and to save time.

In the beginning days of "office automation," the concentration was on clerical and secretarial tasks. Therefore, "word processing" became synonymous with "office automation" or the "office of the future" concept. Stand-alone systems dedicated to word processing began to appear on the market.

And one Canadian company quickly gained credibility in the field.

AES Data Ltd. of Montreal was formed in 1974 by Steven Dorsey as the successor to a company called Automatic Electronic Systems Ltd. The company's literature says it was "a modest size company whose prime assets were a bank of valuable technological expertise in microelectronics plus a sustained, tireless drive to become a significant worldwide force in the burgeoning word processing field."

AES designed, manufactured, and marketed stand-alone systems with financial backing from Innocan Investments Ltd. and in its first year recorded sales of $4 million. In 1978, the Canada Development Corporation (CDC) acquired direct majority control of AES with a 64 per cent share ownership. Lanier Business Products, a U.S.-based manufacturer of office equipment and dictographic recording systems, purchased a one-third interest in AES the same year. The AES products have been marketed worldwide through company-owned sales and services offices. Manufacturing is also done in the United States and West Germany in AES facilities.

Steven Dorsey stepped down from the company presidency in 1978 to start another manufacturing firm, Micom Computer Systems Ltd. He was replaced at AES by John Leng, formerly with Digital Equipment of Canada. Mr. Dorsey took the micro-processor technology he had developed for AES and applied it to another stand-alone word processing system, this one with communications capability.

By 1980, Micom Computer Systems Ltd. had formed a partner-ship with Philips Electronics Ltd. The impetus behind the affilia-tion had been a desire of both partners to add expertise in other areas. Micom had stand-alone word processing units. Philips had computer systems, office products such as dictation units, elec-tronics, communications plus a worldwide marketing organiza-tion.

The world-class technology resident in the AES and Micom organizations has gained a reputation for Canada as a leader in this area. The services offered by such companies as Alphatext Ltd. have also helped to further this reputation.

The area of electronic mail has received a great deal of attention in Canada. I.P. Sharp Associates has developed a serv-ice called "Mailbox" for this purpose, available through the company's worldwide packet switched information network. Both the TransCanada Telephone System and CN/CP Telecom-munications have offered standardized services—Teletex and Infotex respectively—that allow word processors, electronic typewriters, and other office text machines from different man-ufacturers to communicate with each other. TCTS also offers a national store and forward messaging service called Envoy 100.

In early 1982, the Computer Communications Group of the TransCanada Telephone Systems announced a field trial for its iNet Gateway intelligent network concept. To provide more universal accessibility to information providers and other computer-based services, iNet offers a single point of access for the user to a directory of the services offered. From that point, the user can access several services without actually becoming a subscriber of each individual service. More than 30 Canadian information providers made their services available for the trial.

Although much of the "future" technology is here now to make office communications a reality, office automation is still some-what of an infant in the overall scheme of things. User demand and acceptance will be the catalyzing ingredient in the recipe.

2

Hardware: minis and micros prevail

THE COMPUTER HARDWARE industry of the 1970s was characterized by miniaturization.

The semiconductor silicon chip placed all the power of former room-size behemoths on a wafer the size of an average thumbnail. This discovery created a tidal wave of new computer announcements, because the cost of computer technology could now be significantly reduced.

In the United States, a proliferation of minicomputer companies entered the marketplace on the heels of Digital Equipment, Data General, Hewlett-Packard, and Honeywell. Companies like Data 100, Floating Point Systems, Four-Phase Systems, General Automation, Harris Data, MAI (Basic Four), Mohawk Data Sciences, Nixdorf Computer, Olivetti, Perkin-Elmer, Pertec Computer, Prime Computer, Sycor, Texas Instruments, TRW Data Systems, and Wang Laboratories, among others, vied for a piece of the action. The majority began selling on the Canadian scene through distributors or local sales offices in the first half of the decade, although Mohawk had actually begun in the sixties through WM Electronics Ltd.

They were also joined in the minicomputer field by the old standbys—IBM Canada, Burroughs, Control Data, NCR, and Sperry Univac.

The multinational invasion had begun again. But this time, the users were ready for it—and eager for the arrival of the new companies.

By the early 1970s, the computer industry had matured, and the use of the computer had spread. Rather than being just a back-room tool, hidden away from all and sundry, it had become a tool to be used by everyone from clerical staff to management.

The newer machines were much more "user friendly," a term coined to underscore the fact that they could be used by people other than programmers and systems staff. Although some training was needed before operating the machines, generally a few commands in plain English were all that was needed to get into a program and begin to use the computer. The smaller computers no longer needed a special environment, meaning that even small businesses could afford to place a computer system in their offices. Desktop systems and terminals began appearing on the desks of executives as well as secretaries.

The proliferation of computer systems throughout all levels of business had created a demand for more applications software. The applications had moved from general accounting into management related areas: report generation, text management, word processing, data base creation and management, computer graphics, computer-aided design (CAD), computer-aided manufacturing (CAM), communications, and so on. Architects, doctors, engineers, lawyers, and other professionals were among the new breed of users of computer technology. Educational facilities also looked to the new applications such as computer-aided learning (CAL) as a teaching tool.

Computer graphics (whether black and white or colour), CAD/CAM, and related applications fostered another sector of the hardware and software market specializing in these areas. U.S.-based companies like Hewlett-Packard, Tektronix, and Calcomp (California Computer Corp.) became the leaders in the Canadian marketplace as well. However, Canadian companies like Norpak Ltd. and Lektromedia soon found they could share in the wealth of this lucrative field.

Software houses grew up around the hardware industry to supply the ever-increasing demand for customized software programs. As well, standard "off-the-shelf" packages began to appear for specific computer models. The demand for computers and appropriate software was so great that another complete industry sector developed—that of the third party suppliers or OEM (original equipment manufacturer) who would obtain a quantity discount from the manufacturer on the hardware, provide the "value-added" service of supplying customized software for the buyer, and the promise of maintenance as well.

For the computer manufacturer, this segment of the industry was a welcome one. The OEMs could handle sales of single computer systems to the small businesses, leaving the computer firms free to concentrate on sales to the larger users for distributed processing and other multiple system areas. A large number of Canadian computer hardware companies now listed in trade directories belong to this group.

Storage technology had matured as well to the point where computer software programs could now be stored on diskettes—thin sleeved disks reminiscent of 45 r.p.m. records that could be "played" on computers. Recording information on diskettes was a simple function. This new technology greatly facilitated the previously monstrous tasks of information storage and retrieval.

Throughout the seventies, computers became smaller. And the price of hardware steadily decreased. Semiconductor technology had made "micro" computers possible. These miniature computers were initially the domain of the hobbyist and the scientist or engineer. They were first available in kit form to be put together in a "do-it-yourself" manner.

From hobby computing, the microcomputers were soon being called "home" computers—assuming they would be programmed for such household functions as budgeting, financial record keeping (for cheques, payments, etc.), recipe storage and manipulation ("How can I stretch my recipe for two to feed six?" and so on), and finally to play computer games.

Toward the end of the decade, the emphasis for microcomputers again shifted from "home" to "personal." But this time, the concentration was on business. Very small business enterprises, such as restaurants, filling stations, and single-proprietor firms recognized the potential and power of these machines to do their accounting and management reporting functions. For less than half the cost of the smallest of the small business computers, they could have almost the same amount of computing power, capacity, and capability.

This phenomenon resulted in the mushrooming of computer stores all across the country. The stores sold such computer systems as MITS Altair, Apple, Commodore, Cromemco, Imsai, North Star, Processor Technology, TRS-80, Zilog, and a variety of other makes and models. The selection continued to grow throughout the 1970s and the demand for their specific capabilities and size increased.

By the beginning of the 1980s, the microcomputer had become a very sophisticated piece of machinery. Software houses, which had formerly concentrated on programs or packages for mainframe and minicomputer equipment, began to offer packages for micros as well. The amount of software available on the market for the various models of microcomputers made them more attractive to small businesses in particular.

As might have been expected, manufacturers associated with larger computer equipment and office machinery entered the market with microcomputer systems of their own. Xerox was one of the first on the scene with their personal "information processing" system, followed rapidly by IBM, Digital Equipment, Hewlett-Packard, Canon, and Victor. Others (such as NCR and Olivetti) are expected to follow suit as the demand for this type of computer system for business use increases.

"The whole market has come full circle," says Denny Doyle, now president of NABU Manufacturing Ltd. of Ottawa. "If you look in the computer trade journals today, you'll see people selling modules, just the way I was doing back in 1963. Computer systems can be put together by buying parts. The 'mini' computers of today are really the micros. In the same way, they started in the scientific side and have moved into business."

A third chance at manufacturing

The development of the semiconductor chip by Intel provided yet another opportunity for Canada to get into hardware manufacturing.

Micro Computer Machines (MCM) Inc. was formed in 1972 by Mers Kutt within a year after he had left Consolidated Computer Inc. The first and most remembered product developed by Micro Computer Machines was the MCM 800 desktop computer.

It was, according to Mr. Kutt, the first commercial computer product to use a microprocessor chip—the Intel 8008.

"When we first demonstrated it," says Mr. Kutt, "it really shocked a lot of people. IBM officials, Intel, and others were really impressed by it. They didn't believe that this little chip they were producing could do that much. We were the first to do what others like Apple did later in the seventies. We built our own circuit board using the first 8-bit chip in the world.

"When I was with Consolidated, I met with Bob Noyce who, along with Gordon Moore, was one of the founders of the California-based Intel Corporation. They had just developed a 4-bit calculator chip for some Japanese firm. I told him I wanted an 8-bit chip to use in one of the Consolidated systems. He mentioned that they had thought about designing one, but the Board of Directors had rejected the idea because of the expense.

"We talked about Consolidated possibly providing some funding to help in the development of the chip, and took the idea back to our respective Boards. Mine agreed that it looked like a good avenue to pursue. But when I called Mr. Noyce the next week, he said that Intel had decided to finance the project alone. Soon after that, I left Consolidated and formed MCM."

The MCM computer was one of the first non-IBM machines to incorporate APL as one of the programming languages. It was also a leader in the area of integrated word processing.

Micro Computer Machines has gone through a number of changes in the past decade. Within two years, the Board of Directors had appointed a receiver, even though it was (according to Mr. Kutt) not in financial trouble. The Board ended up buying half of Mers Kutt's shares (at, he says, a very depressed value) and he was asked to step down from the presidency of the company.

MCM did not go bankrupt at that time. Under subsequent presidents Chuck Williams (now with Geac Canada Ltd.) and John Woods, the company continued product development in the microcomputer area. However, in recent years, MCM distributed U.S. and Japanese products rather than continuing to manufacture. A receiver was appointed in June 1982.

Consolidated Computer Inc., meanwhile, had entered the 1970s riding the crest of a high technology wave. With domestic and international sales going well and new products being researched, no one within the company could have predicted the topsy-turvy future that lay ahead for Consolidated.

At the turn of the decade, negotiations were begun with both International Computers Limited (ICL) of England and Fujitsu Ltd. of Japan for reciprocal marketing of each other's products in their respective countries. At the same time, Consolidated Computer was talking to the General Adjustment Assistance Board (GAAB) of the Canadian federal government for financial support. "We had wanted some sort of lease financing arrangement," says Mers Kutt, "but the government didn't have a vehicle for that type of agreement."

Consolidated Computer worked out a line of financing with GAAB whereby the company would receive 80 per cent of the first $15 million worth of equipment it installed. "To get that $12 million, we installed $15 million worth of equipment, and even had our salesmen go back into the field to re-sign contracts for equipment we had previously sold," says Mr. Kutt. "But the full amount of the financing never did come through. We received only about $6 million from GAAB."

Consolidated was placed in receivership in 1971 by GAAB and its chairman, Anthony Hampson (now chairman of the Canada Development Corporation). Mers Kutt and Don Pamenter were asked to leave the company. Bill Hutchison was promoted to the position of president and, at the end of 1972, Bill Moore was brought on board as chairman for Consolidated Computer.

The company's history over the next 10 years is somewhat convoluted. Fujitsu acquired some equity in the company in 1972. The Ontario Development Corporation provided funding in addition to that already being received from GAAB. In early 1976, negotiations were under way for control of Consolidated to pass from the Ontario and federal governments to Central Dynamics Ltd. of Montreal (a division of Control Data Canada, Ltd.).

Shares in Consolidated and Comterm Inc. (a Central Dynamic subsidiary) were to be exchanged as part of the deal. The company was restructured with Leslie Sellmeyer, who had been a vice president with Central Dynamics, being brought in as president of Consolidated. The negotiations fell through, but

Sellmeyer remained as president until the company was sold by the governments to NABU Manufacturing Ltd. of Ottawa in 1982.

In that sale, a 64 per cent interest in Consolidated was sold to NABU for $1, plus a related payment of $100,000 in cash (to absorb CCI's debt of nearly $50 million) plus an expected $7 million in participating payments over the next five years. Fujitsu still held some 24 per cent interest in the company at the time this book was compiled.

Consolidated's revenues roller-coastered over the years. In the years prior to its sale—although revenues were good—the company chalked up large losses. Its product line was reduced, leaving only the Key-Edit 2000 and lottery terminal products. It is estimated that keeping the company afloat over the years has cost the Canadian and Ontario taxpayers about $125 million.

There are many questions about Consolidated Computer Inc. that may never be answered. Was there conflict of interest or political patronage at various stages in the company's history? Could Consolidated Computer have become the symbol of Canada's technology-based future? What will its future be?

But that's the subject for a book by itself.

One company with a success story in Canadian manufacturing is Geac Canada Limited of Toronto, started in April 1971 by R. A. (Gus) German and Robert Isserstedt. Gus German had been part of the team of third-year University of Waterloo students (along with Richard Shirley, now senior vice president of Comterm Inc.) who developed the WATFOR (Waterloo Fortran) computer software program.

Geac did not begin manufacturing until 1976. Until then, the company ordered its hardware from outside suppliers, manufacturing only the interfaces. Geac was basically an OEM, providing software programming as well in a language the owners called Our Programming Language (OPL).

While the Geac 8000 computer system was still on the drawing board, Real Time Datapro Ltd. of Toronto signed a commitment for the first machine.

"The computer was still spread all over the work bench in the Geac lab," says Real Time president Gerry Meinzer. "But we felt that Geac would be able to deliver a good hardware product. It was a major risk, but we calculated the risk very carefully. We looked at it for a number of reasons—the cycles, the economic benefits. We had the concept for an insurance program on the shelf for quite some time. Be we didn't have the right kind of hardware product in the marketplace to do exactly what we wanted to do—except for the system that Geac was designing. We set up our own software on the machine, which was one month late in arriving off the bench, and within a year we were competitive with an American software product that ran on IBM equipment and that our competitors were using."

Geac also developed its 9000 online banking system which incorporated EFTS (electronic funds transfer systems), packet switching, automated teller machines, and OCR (optical character recognition) wands. Today, a large number of Geac's clients are in the banking industry.

The company is also very active in Europe, and began a joint venture in England with Real Time Datapro Limited early in 1982. Geac's Board of Directors have formed a business development and management umbrella called Geac Computers International Inc. to oversee activities of the subsidiaries in Canada, England, and the United States as well as marketing in other countries around the world.

Manufacturing of terminals and terminal products is one area in which Canadian companies in the computer field have done extremely well. One such company is Comterm Inc. of Montreal, formed in 1970 by Richard Shirley and Yens Larsen. The idea for the company was formulated when Mr. Shirley and Mr. Larsen worked for Computel Systems Limited. When they decided to form their own company, Central Dynamics Limited provided the funding. Comterm is one of the high technology companies that have taken advantage of the stock market's interest in computer investment, receiving a listing on the Toronto Stock Exchange in May, 1982.

Comterm Inc. underwent a management change in 1978, at which time Laurent Nadeau became president of the company and Richard Shirley became senior vice president.

Another group of University of Waterloo graduates led by Mike Volker and Ron Craig formed Kitchener-based Volker-Craig Limited in 1973 to design and manufacture video display terminals. In addition to a range of microprocessor-based terminals marketed under the Volker-Craig name, the company also manufactured terminals under licence to Courier Terminal Systems of Phoenix, Arizona. A successful company, Volker-Craig was purchased in 1982 by NABU Manufacturing.

In Montreal in 1970, Peter Carey started a company called Lektromedia to manufacture interactive computer systems based on a video display terminal with graphics capability and audio-visual inputs he had developed. With some research support from the National Research Council, Lektromedia developed the technology and software support for a series of computer-aided learning computer systems that have been widely used in Canada. The company moved its headquarters to Belleville, Ont., in 1979.

Cybernex Ltd., which manufactures a digitizer video terminal, was formed in Ottawa in 1974 by Jim Gadzala, Colin Turner and Bruce Douglas. A fourth partner, Dave Londry, joined the firm somewhat later.

Other companies across Canada have begun manufacturing computer hardware components and subsystems as well as complete microcomputer systems. Electrohome Limited of Kitchener, Northern Technologies Ltd. (a joint venture of Northern Telecom Ltd. and Lanpar Technologies Inc. of Toronto), Patrick Computer Systems of Winnipeg, Network Data Systems Ltd. of Toronto, and Remanco Systems Inc. of Toronto are examples of the technological know-how that exists in Canada. Others have been mentioned in the chapter on data communications.

Mainframes and plug compatibles

The activity among the large multinational mainframe manufacturers—the original "Snow White and the Seven Dwarfs"—continued on throughout the decade, marked mainly by the failure of three of the original nine companies and the entry of the survivors into the minicomputer and microcomputer markets.

In 1970, General Electric sold its worldwide operations to Honeywell. In Canada, the merger of Canadian General Electric and Honeywell's computer and communications groups resulted in the formation of the Honeywell Information Systems division.

In 1976, Honeywell also acquired the computer customer base worldwide of Xerox Corporation. About the same time, RCA divested itself of its computer division to concentrate on other areas of business.

Both Xerox and General Electric re-entered the computer business somewhat later with terminals, printers, and personal computers.

Perhaps the most important announcement of the seventies was the start-up of Amdahl Limited in the United States in 1970 by Dr. Gene Amdahl, the man who had created the architecture for the 360 family of computers while working for IBM. He had an idea for a new computer system that IBM rejected. He then set out to design and manufacture the system himself. Completely compatible with the existing IBM architecture, the Amdahl 470V/6 soon captured the imagination of the computer buying public.

In 1976, the Canadian operation of Amdahl opened with Ted White as president. Mr. White left the AGT division of Multiple Access that year to take on this new challenge.

"When we started in Canada, I was the only employee," says Mr. White. "Now we have a $75 million business and about 200 employees. It's a very different business now from what it was then, with a completely new set of management requirements.

"Amdahl's market share in Canada in 1982 in the large systems business is about one-third—*i.e.* one-third of all the large mainframe systems installed in the country. That's more than twice what it is in the United States. The Canadian marketplace appears more willing than the U.S. market to accept compatible solutions. The other big companies in the IBM compatible market are Memorex and Storage Technology, both with large disk drives and subsystems. Both have done extremely well in Canada, cornering about two-thirds of the IBM disk market."

The success of firms like Amdahl, Memorex, and Storage Technology in Canada points to a willingness among users (particularly of IBM equipment) to opt for a "multi-vendor" data centre in which they can get a totally compatible environment without relying on one vendor to supply the equipment. This flexibility is attractive to many users, especially those with large computing centres, who can now shop for the best prices, capabilities, and delivery dates without leaving the IBM fold.

Within the next few years, many more companies like Itel (now National Advanced Systems) had also entered Canada selling IBM compatible mainframe computer systems.

By the end of the decade, and on into the eighties, there was still a requirement—by the large organizations such as the airlines, banks, insurance companies, universities and others— for multi-processor mainframe computer systems. As their data processing needs grew, so did the size of the systems they ordered.

3

Consolidation hits computing services firms

*T*HE *FRENETIC ACTIVITY* in the computer services area during the sixties, and the intense competition that followed, led to a change in the character of the industry during the seventies and early eighties.

Some of the pioneer companies continued to maintain their corporate identities, and a few small entrepreneurial service firms entered the business scene for the first time. However, a new breed of service company began to move toward centre stage. These newcomers were either well-funded joint efforts of existing commercial enterprises, or government owned and operated organizations.

In addition, some of the companies formed in the sixties had outgrown their fledgling entrepreneurial stages to become more mature businesses requiring more professional management skills.

"There was no room for a medium-sized organization," says Ted White. "You either had to be very small and localized or very large and national."

As a result, there was a move toward consolidation. In the computer services industry, mergers increasingly became the order of the decade.

An examination of the industry during the period should begin, perhaps, with a survey of some of the survivors of the sixties.

I.P. Sharp Associates

Under the capable leadership of Ian Sharp, I.P. Sharp Associates continued to expand nationally and internationally. In 1973, the company opened an office in London, England. Three years later, the Ottawa-based hardware division of the company was sold to a group of employees who formed Goodwood Data Systems. The parent continued to concentrate on software and international network development plans.

The I.P. Sharp international APL-based packet switching network was introduced in 1976. With the installation of a second Amdahl 470V/6 II mainframe in 1979, the company became the largest commercial APL timesharing facility in the world.

By the early 1980s, the I.P. Sharp network spanned the globe. The company had opened offices in Europe, Australia, the United States, Mexico, and the Far East as well as throughout Canada. Clients in more than 500 cities around the world have local telephone access to the Sharp Toronto facilities. The company provides a wide range of public data bases and business applications packages programmed and processed in APL.

"We started as a software company, and that's what we still are," Mr. Sharp says succinctly. "By using our software, clients can also connect their own data centres to our network. No other company in the world offers that capability. About 25 data centres, scattered about the world, are connected to the [Sharp] network."

A U.S. observer has called I.P. Sharp Associates "the bellwether and template of how this sort of company should be run in the future." With exports accounting for more than 70 per cent of the company's gross sales, I.P. Sharp Associates is Canada's largest exporter of computer services.

Computel Systems Ltd.

At Computel, although revenues continued to climb steadily, expenses were also mounting. In 1970, the company acquired Information Systems Design Inc. (ISD) of California. ISD was operating a Univac 1108 to provide the San Francisco market area with services similar to those offered by Computel. This acquisition enabled Computel to discontinue the unprofitable Toronto 1108 data centre and subsequently to establish new facilities in Montreal. However, by the end of 1973, although revenues were at an all time high, the company's net financial position was still precarious, and additional support was needed.

At the same time, the Royal Trust Company was reassessing its computer operations. A number of meetings between Computel and Royal Trust officials led to an agreement under which Computel would supply Royal Trust with computing services and Royal Trust would acquire a 20 per cent equity in Computel. Later, this equity was increased to 51 per cent, and at the end of 1975, Royal Trust was in possession of about 95 per cent of Computel shares.

By the end of 1974, the Royal Trust computer work load had been transferred to the Computel system. During the same year, Computel acquired Data Logic Canada Ltd., which had begun operations in 1971, providing application programming services and a proprietary programming system, Mark IV.

The association with Royal Trust and the acquisition of Data Logic with its application packages, enabled Computel to develop a nation-wide computer service network, based in Ottawa, with branches across Canada. The company continued to diversify its client base, increasing the number of its private sector clients.

In the mid-seventies, when Royal Trust began operations in Florida, ISD expanded into the banking and financial services in that state. The move was to prove fatal to ISD's future as a Computel subsidiary. Under the regulations of the U.S. Bank Holding Companies Act, the U.S. Federal Reserve Board ordered the divestiture of ISD from Royal Trust.

When Computel celebrated its 10th anniversary in 1977, the company reported a net profit of $940,000 for the six-month period ending June 30, and revenues that were 29 per cent higher than in the preceding year. In 1979, the company acquired SDI Associates from London Life Insurance Company, with which SDI had been affiliated since 1976.

However, by 1980, Computel, although ranking third among Canadian computing service companies in revenues, was again being plagued by net losses. A year later it recovered, recording a profit. In April of 1981, the Data Logic division was sold. In 1982, Computel was acquired by one of the seventies newcomers, Canada Systems Group.

Dataline Systems Ltd.

By the early seventies, Dataline was beginning to change business direction, from supplying clients with computer cycles to providing value-added, result-oriented services. Joe Paradi could foresee an increasing demand by what he calls "the general ledger type people" for computer-based applications such as accounts payable, accounts receivable, and invoicing.

"To reach this market, we had to change our original way of doing business and our own thinking processes," Dr. Paradi says. "Instead of going to someone who was an engineer or programmer or statistical analyst and talking about the computer system, we had to talk to people who were not technically oriented but just wanted to get their work done. Our salesmen could no longer bend the bits and bytes, but had to be able to understand the customer's business and to analyze the customer's requirements. Our technical people could find a computer solution only if the marketing group related the appropriate facts."

With this change in marketing approach, the era of the salesman as "high technology priest" ended at Dataline, and the implementation of "user friendly" systems and software packages began.

By the late seventies, only 20 per cent of Dataline's business was providing cycles. Its market areas included timesharing services, socio-economic services, online data base management, and business data processing.

According to Dr. Paradi, Dataline has been unique in its approach to providing services through low-speed keyboard-driven terminals. "For all practical purposes, the clerk who enters the sales order is operating the computer," he says. "This means that a people-oriented outlook has been very important. You don't have to be a master mechanic to drive a car. Similarly, you don't have to be a master programmer to make use of the services we provide."

Dataline became profitable in 1973, and throughout the seventies continued to grow. Offices were opened in Ottawa, Montreal, Winnipeg, Calgary, and Vancouver. In 1975, the company was invited to list its common shares with the Toronto Stock Exchange. Four years later, it expanded operations outside

Canada with the establishment of DSL Systems Inc. in New York to serve the United States market. A computer communications network linked operations across Canada and parts of the U.S. The original Digital Equipment PDP-10 installation had grown to a multiple installation of DECsystem-10 computers.

In 1980, the business path Dataline had been following so smoothly became a bit rough. During that fiscal year, the company suffered a net loss due primarily, according to the annual report, to "our heavy investment in our U.S. subsidiary, DSL Systems Inc." Dataline closed down its U.S. operations, and by 1982 Dr. Paradi was able to report to the company's shareholders that Dataline was "back on the profit trail."

Systems Dimensions Ltd.

In the early seventies, SDL swung into an acquisitions mode. In order to sell computing services to the Quebec government, the company needed a Quebec City base for business. SDL broke off the agency agreement it had maintained with AGT Data Services and acquired Informatel, a small software development company that had been operating in Quebec. SDL Informatique, with offices in Quebec City and Montreal, was formed.

Next, SDL looked south to the United States market, acquiring EDP Industries of White Plains, New York, to create SDL International. Eventually, offices were opened in Boston, New York City, and Washington.

Further acquisition broadened the scope of services provided. Softwarehouse, an Ottawa-based software development organization headed by Jack Davies, joined the SDL fold. Toronto-based Systems Research Group Inc., which had pioneered the development of information analysis research and applications, especially in education and health care, became part of SDL in 1972. SRG was headed by Dr. Jack Levine and Professor Richard Judy. On the basis of this acquisition, the SDL Institute was established to provide policy and economic research, cost benefit analyses, and educational programs.

"We began to think of SDL as the information think-tank for Canada," George Fierheller says.

He also planned to expand and further diversify the market served by SDL. "Our belief was that the new services we were developing could be delivered to the home and office by cable," he says. "The idea was not new, but we were going to be the first to put it into practice in North America."

To provide these kinds of services, SDL struck a deal with Ottawa Cablevision Limited, contingent upon CRTC approval. The hearing took place in June, 1974. "The decision has become a Canadian classic," Mr. Fierheller says. "The CRTC simply stated that such a merger for these purposes was 'premature'."

Despite this decision, SDL continued to grow, and with growth came change. Jack Davies left to form Systemhouse Limited, which was to become one of Canada's largest software development firms. Jack Levine and Richard Judy resigned, and with their departure the Systems Research Group program ended. However, by 1975 the company was bringing in more than $21 million in sales, and realizing a profit of more than $1 million. By 1977, SDL itself was a target for acquisition.

At that time, both Datacrown and Sun Life made offers, but it was a third company, Coastal Enterprises Ltd. of Nova Scotia, that won the day. For about a year, SDL operated as a wholly-owned subsidiary of Coastal Enterprises, and under the new ownership began to make further acquisitions. In 1978, SDL acquired a profitable western subsidiary, ADP Systems Limited, a Winnipeg service company that had been started by Dave Cortens.

The same year, Datacrown—as will be recounted later in this chapter—made an offer that Coastal Enterprises didn't refuse.

Real Time Datapro Ltd.

Real Time Datapro Ltd. came to life in its present incarnation in 1974, although (as was mentioned in Part One of this book) the companies that gave birth to it boasted a history going back to 1876. At that time, a company called Library Bureau offered specialized tabulating and statistical services to insurance companies in Montreal and Toronto. "It had started out with library cards, tabulating who takes out what kind of books," says Real Time president Gerhard (Gerry) Meinzer, "then went on to develop insurance statistics with equipment that was just one step faster than a hand crank. When we took over the division, we took over a lot of these accounts. That's why we could offer to one of our long standing accounts service continuity of more than 50 years."

Library Bureau became part of Recording and Statistical Company, a division of Sperry-Rand in the 1930s.

Datapro Limited was a service firm based in London, Ont., begun in 1962 to offer computerized write-up services and income tax services to professional accountants. Datapro operated mainly in the southwestern Ontario region and also had an office in Windsor.

"In the early days, geography was very important," says Mr. Meinzer. "It wasn't as easy to move stuff across the wires. You had to bring in your punch cards or your source documents and have them punched up. There was a fair amount of business in the London area, and Datapro found it could harvest that particular geographical corner. Nowadays, a company could just as easily be in London as Toronto. Communications no longer dictate that you have to be in a specific spot."

Real Time Corporation Limited had been formed in 1969 and in 1971 had acquired the Toronto offices of Recording and Statistical Company. Gerry Meinzer came on board as president at this time, after a professional career that had included working for IBM Canada and Grace Computer Services. Also in 1971, the Montreal offices of Recording and Statistical Company went to Welby Computer Services. Welby, whose head office was in Ottawa, was acquired by Real Time Datapro in 1978.

In 1974, Datapro Limited purchased Real Time Corporation in a reverse takeover and the companies were consolidated into Real Time Datapro Ltd.

Real Time Datapro is active in general insurance, municipal government, and accountancy systems mainly in Ontario and Quebec. The company utilizes Geac computer equipment, obtaining the first Geac computer manufactured, as it came off the line in 1976.

In July, 1981, Real Time created a joint venture company with Geac computers in London, England, called Real Time Insurance Systems, to provide computer-based insurance packages to the general insurance industry throughout Western Europe. The company will make use of the combined hardware/software expertise of its two Canadian parents with Real Time's Policy

Management Systems software and Geac's 6000 and 8000 line of computers.

In the fiscal year ended February, 1981, Real Time Datapro reported revenues of just over $5 million, an increase of some 18 per cent over the previous year. In 1982, reporting revenues for the 1981 fiscal year, Real Time was looking at a real growth of about 21 per cent, with profit growth of approximately 50 per cent.

The new breed of service companies

Early in the seventies, two service companies that were to become dominating forces in the industry were formed. Those two were Canada Systems Group Limited and Datacrown Inc.

Canada Systems Groups Limited began as a joint venture involving three major Canadian corporations and one United States based company. The original partners of The Canada Systems Group (ELST) Limited were the T. Eaton Company Limited, London Life Insurance Company, and Steel Company of Canada Limited. The U.S. partner was TRW Inc., headquartered in Cleveland, Ohio.

Pooling data processing hardware and personnel, these companies reasoned, would cut in-house data processing costs. Providing computer services to outside clients would enable them to diversify their business operations. TRW was also interested in establishing a strong Canadian presence.

"Canada Systems Group was not just another data centre, offering processing capabilities," comments an industry observer. "They also provided application programming support to the primary partners. Through TRW's participation, they became involved with the engineering and high technology field. This was a major move in the data processing industry."

In 1971, William Boggs, president of Litton Industries and former president of de Havilland Aircraft of Canada, was appointed president of the new company, now incorporated as The Canada Systems Group (EST) Limited.

"Bill Boggs is a professional manager," a colleague says. "He has a strong personal image, strong personal contacts, and is clearly a senior executive by any standards. His right-hand man, Cam Bright (vice president, processing services group), came from

Eaton's managerial ranks, a manager who understands the applications of computing. They've provided sound leadership to CSG."

Shortly after Mr. Boggs joined CSG, the ground was broken for the company's building in Mississauga, Ontario. By October of 1971, the first processor—an IBM System 370 Model 155—was installed and began the first run of Stelco processing on the Thanksgiving weekend, A few months later, a second similar processor was installed.

Before operations had even begun, London Life withdrew from the consortium. Further changes occurred in 1974, with the withdrawal of TRW and the entrance of Gulf Canada as an equal partner.

However, by early 1972, the conversion of the "equity customers" (Eaton's and Stelco) had been completed and in October of that year the first non-equity client, Abitibi Paper Company, was signed. During the initial year of operations, $6 million of business was generated.

Almost immediately, CSG embarked on the first in a series of acquisitions that would make the company a top supplier of computing services in Canada. In 1973, CSG acquired Digital Methods Limited of Ottawa, and in 1974 opened an Ottawa branch in the DML building. In 1975, L&W Data Systems of Toronto (formed by Mike Lucas and Dennis Wray) became a CSG subsidiary, providing the company with an entry into minicomputers and turnkey business systems. Cogito, a supplier of educational data processing services, based in Princeton, New Jersey, joined CSG in 1978. The same year, CSG acquired Eric Moss and Associates of Montreal, which became the headquarters for CSG's first Montreal office. Annual corporate revenues were now in excess of $27 million.

However, perhaps the most significant acquisition occurred in 1979 when, by acquiring the Multiple Access Computer Group, CSG almost doubled in size.

In the preceding years, Multiple Access had been acquiring smaller computer service firms, such as AGT Data Services and Comserve Ltd. The acquisitions enabled the company to offer services both on Control Data equipment (from the original Multiple Access) and IBM equipment (from AGT). It still tended to have a scientifically-oriented strategy, largely because of its use of Control Data equipment, and became known throughout the industry as *the* non-IBM bureau.

An additional acquisition was Greyhound Computing Corp. of Los Angeles. Multiple Access had expanded its operations to include branches across Canada and in San Francisco, California. In time, however, Cemp Investments, who controlled Multiple Access, began diversifying its interests into broadcasting. Subsequently, the computer sector of the company was sold to Canada Systems Group.

President Boggs calls the acquisition of Multiple Access Computer Group "one of the most exciting" developments of the company's history. "It happened so quickly, just about three weeks from the time we really decided to go. We had enormous support from the owners."

The corporate name was changed to Canada Systems Group Limited. By 1981, CSG annual sales had risen to $100 million, to make it the top revenue producer among Canadian computing services organizations. A Western Region processing centre was opened in Calgary, and the company introduced a new line of CSG NUTAK minicomputers.

The acquisition of Computel Systems Ltd. from Royal Trust in 1982 further increased Canada Systems Group's size and scope, offering new potential for future corporate development.

Datacrown Inc.

What president Richard Taylor disarmingly describes as "an interesting idea" sparked a chain of events that resulted in the formation of Datacrown Ltd. in 1971.

By 1969, employee-owned SDI Associates had established its expertise in providing consulting and software services for insurance companies and was ready for further expansion. Mr. Taylor and A.J. (Tony) Simms had joined SDI during that year.

"Basically, the idea was to get a number of large insurance companies together," Mr. Taylor says. "They would put all their data processing into one centre, SDI would install large computers to do their work, and very likely we'd be able to do other people's processing as well. I don't know who in the group first came up with the concept of totally replacing in-house computers, which eventually became Datacrown's major area of concentration."

The numbers for such a joint venture made sense, he says. With the economies of scale possible in the envisioned operation, costs to clients for processing data would be 20 to 30 per cent less than for doing the work on their own equipment.

SDI invited five Canadian life insurance companies to a meeting in Toronto to discuss the plan. (Crown Life was not one of the five.) Three of those who heard the presentation thought they'd like to be counted in, and agreed to back an in-depth study. Dick Taylor and Tony Simms went to work on the project.

One of the original three companies dropped out, but in 1970 Crown Life expressed interest in the venture. "Jasper Moore was vice president of Crown Life at the time," Mr. Taylor recalls. "Bruce Campbell (SDI president) went up to Jasper's cottage to chat with him, and then Bruce and I made a call at Jasper's office. Crown Life's willingness to go ahead was a real high for me. I'd never been a salesman, and that was something we sold."

He and Mr. Simms updated the plan, now basing their business calculations on the use of the newly announced IBM 370 series. One by one, the other companies withdrew from the proposed consortium, until in early 1971 only Crown Life remained. Crown offered to buy SDI, but the company turned down the offer. "Within 24 hours, SDI was faced with two business opportunities that were mutually exclusive," Mr. Taylor says. "One was the Crown bid. We had an SDI executive meeting to discuss the alternatives, and the decision was made to opt for the other opportunity. While I wasn't happy about it, I understood why."

However, he was still unwilling to let the matter drop. "The day after SDI decided not to proceed, I talked to Tony Simms and asked if he'd be willing to split the cost of a lunch to talk the matter over with one of the Crown Life people and see whether the company would be interested in going ahead," Mr. Taylor recalls.

Tony Simms was indeed willing. In a small restaurant south of Bloor Street, the proposal for the formation of a computer services subsidiary company was put to Alan Morson, then superintendent of data systems for Crown, now executive vice president, insurance operations. Mr. Morson listened carefully, and that afternoon he called Dick Taylor to say that Crown Life wanted to pursue the idea further.

During the following weeks, working together after hours late into the night at Mr. Simms' apartment, Mr. Taylor, Mr. Simms, and Mr. Morson put together a complete business plan for the new company. The first time the proposal went before the Crown Life Board, it was turned back with the request for more information. Full details were then presented by Crown president Rob Dowsett to the directors, and on May 20, 1971, the Board approved the plan.

"After meeting with the Board that day, I waited while they considered their verdict," Dick Taylor recalls. "I can still see the tracks I wore in the carpet as I paced the floor. When the good news came, I couldn't find Tony—he was out grocery shopping. But we finally got together, and he and his fiancée (now his wife), my wife and I opened a bottle of champagne to celebrate."

Dick Taylor and Tony Simms resigned from SDI and a week later began working at Crown Life to put their plan into action.

"We joined Crown to start Datacrown with the clear understanding that it would be set up as a separate company, and that we would do all of Crown's computer work on an arm's length basis," Mr. Taylor says. "They would put up the original financing, but Datacrown would be run as a separate company. Our mandate was to provide a total alternative to an in-house computer. And we didn't focus on anything else for a number of years."

He credits Dave Carlisle, now president of Infomart, with coining the term "Shared Processing" to describe Datacrown's basic concept.

Shared Processing builds on the principle of achieving economies and improved productivity in data processing through the sharing of a large-scale general purpose computing complex. "Datacrown would provide the leading-edge computing power, the telecommunications facilities, and the technical support to meet the full data processing needs of all our clients all the time," Mr. Taylor says.

"I was told that Datacrown would never work, for two reasons. First, we'd never be able to figure out how to convert customers from the small IBM operating system (DOS, disk operating system) to the big operating system (OS). Second, SDL would not sell us the software product it had developed for accounting for the resource use on a big system. Without that accounting capability, we were told, we couldn't be in business.

"However, we did figure out how to convert DOS to OS. And we bought a basic accounting system in the U.S., modified the hell out of it, and used it as the basis of our accounting system. It worked just fine."

Meanwhile, Mr. Taylor set about recruiting staff for the new company. David Carlisle came to Datacrown from AGT Data Services' Montreal operations. "He had been marketing the services of SDL and had already concluded that there was a market for replacing in-house computers," Mr. Taylor says. "I didn't have to sell him on the idea; he was already committed."

From IBM, Montreal, came Bill Harker to be vice president, research and development. He spent 3 years at Datacrown, later moving to the Bank of Montreal as a senior vice president.

Mr. Carlisle lured Gordon Lucas from IBM's Ottawa office "by describing the endless problems to be solved." Mr. Lucas is now group vice president of data systems for Datacrown, responsible for the control of technology and for the operation of the company's three Systemcenters.

The first Datacrown Ltd. Systemcenter opened for operation in the Toronto suburb of Willowdale in June 1972, with an IBM System 370 Model 165 processor. Services offered included program development aids, data entry, data base management, file maintenance, report generators, information retrieval systems, and management service packages. The company's first contracts were with AGT Data Services, the Bank of Nova Scotia, and Crown Life. Processing for the first two was under way before the work for Crown Life began.

Revenues for the first year were $1 million. By 1976, the company's first profitable year, they had reached $16 million. In January 1978, the company announced 1977 revenues of $20 million with a profit of $1.7 million. By this time, Datacrown had established branch offices in Ottawa and Vancouver, and had replaced more than 50 in-house computers to become the largest supplier of remote computing services in Canada. Computer facilities had expanded in Toronto with the acquisition of the first IBM System 370 Model 168 in Canada. The company had also begun operations in the United States, with clients in Atlanta, Georgia. In 1978, a branch office was opened in Dallas, Texas.

"Not everything we touched turned to gold," Mr. Taylor says candidly. "As a joint venture with the Bank of Nova Scotia, we started a separate company called Telaccount in August of 1973. It offered accounting services to small companies, who would input their accounting transactions *via* telephone lines, and the next morning would pick up the processed reports at branches of the Bank of Nova Scotia.

"Telaccount was not the success we had hoped it would be."

Datacrown invested about $1.5 million in the venture, and by 1974 more funds were required to make it operate successfully. Mr. Taylor sold Datacrown's interest to the Bank of Nova Scotia for $2. "It was an expensive education for me," he comments.

Eventually, Telaccount was sold to Comtech Group International, and is still part of that company's organization.

More promising were the negotiations for the acquisition of Systems Dimensions Limited. A number of discussions about a possible merger had taken place between Dick Taylor and George Fierheller as early as 1976. As has been noted, in 1977 Coastal Enterprises won the day. However, a year later there were indications that an acquisition was again a possibility.

"I had been terribly disappointed when we failed in our bid for SDL the first time," Dick Taylor says. "In July 1978, for the first time since Datacrown started, I was taking a month off. Shortly before leaving with my family to go camping in Western Canada, I knew we might have an opportunity to buy SDL. We went on our trip, but I kept making telephone calls from the farthest wilds of British Columbia to keep in touch with what was going on.

"There were a number of reasons why we really wanted to get together with SDL. We knew there was going to be a rationalization of the Canadian services industry, and SDL was our first choice for consolidation. We had a high regard for the SDL people, products, and reputation. In addition, we wanted to expand our U.S. operations. SDL was active in the U.S., and they were an approved supplier to the U.S. government. A merger would double our size, giving us a strong Canadian base for U.S. operations.

"And finally, we had expanded very rapidly in 1978 and needed another Systemcenter. SDL had a data centre with growth capability in Ottawa."

In October 1978, the Crown Life Board approved the merger, and Systems Dimensions Limited was joined with Datacrown Ltd. to form Datacrown Inc. George Fierheller stayed on as vice chairman of the Board of Directors until March 1979, when he left to join Premier Cablevision Co. Ltd. in Vancouver as president.

With the merger, Datacrown Inc. became one of the largest computing services companies in North America, and for a time the largest in Canada. Systemcenters were located in Toronto and Ottawa with branch offices in Quebec City, Montreal, Ottawa, Toronto, Winnipeg, Calgary, Vancouver, Boston, New York, Washington, D.C., and Dallas.

"When we bought SDL, our revenues for calendar 1978 were about $28 million and theirs were about $22 million," Mr. Taylor says. "The combined operation made us suddenly a $50 million company."

He adds that there were difficulties in joining two companies that were essentially the same size. "Our control systems, our management systems were not adequate for our increased size. The bad news for 1979 was that at first we didn't really have a management game plan, and we broke even that year. The good news was that we kept our focus on our clients and grew 20 per cent."

By the end of the decade, Datacrown Inc. revenues had reached $60 million, and in the early 1980s they exceeded $86 million. In April 1982, the company's Washington, D.C., Systemcenter was officially opened, the first computer centre to be built in the U.S. by a Canadian company.

On Datacrown's 10th anniversary, president Taylor could report that the company was serving 1,000 clients in Canada and the U.S., had replaced nearly 100 computer systems, and anticipated 1982 revenues of more than $90 million.

The formation of Datacrown had indeed proved to be "an interesting idea."

Meanwhile, the company where the idea had originated had undergone some changes. After the negotiations with Crown Life were terminated, SDI Associates started offering its facilities management services to Industrial Acceptance Corporation. In 1976, an affiliation was formed with London Life Insurance Company through which SDI took over all the in-house data processing for London Life in addition to its work with outside clients. In 1979, that partnership dissolved and SDI operations were taken over by Computel Systems Limited. Because of this merger, SDI became a part of Canada Systems Group when Computel was acquired by CSG in 1982.

Other newcomers in the seventies

In Quebec, Ducros, Meilleur, Roy et Associés (DMR) was founded in 1973 by three IBM Montreal graduates to provide computer software and consulting services.

"Pierre Ducros and Serge Meilleur were two young supersalesmen," a colleague recalls. "Alain Roy was a talented consultant. The three complemented each other and constituted a superb team. They were also intelligent—they asked Bernard Côté to be one of the company's directors. Bernie was older and was a very good, experienced businessman. DMR filled the vacuum that had been left with the decline of BST."

One of the company's first major projects was creating a system to manage the results of the 1976 Summer Olympic Games. Six years later, DMR had grown to an organization employing more than 500 people, with branch offices across Canada and in the United States. Recently, annual sales reached $27 million, and the company is widely respected throughout the industry for the caliber of its services.

Also in Quebec, the Industrial Life Insurance Co. of Quebec City formed IST Industrial Life Technical Services Inc. in 1974. Phil Lemay, former IBM vice president, data processing for Eastern Canada, was appointed president of the new company, which was headquartered in Montreal. By 1976, IST had branches in Quebec City and Ottawa, and in 1977 further expanded with the acquisition of Société de Mathématiques Appliquées.

In 1980, Industrial Life insurance executive Maurice Martel

was appointed president and chief executive officer of what has become Quebec's largest computer services company. Phil Lemay left the company that year to join Amdahl in Paris, France.

A year later, it was announced that IST was teaming up with Winnipeg-based Cybershare, broadening the computer capabilities of both companies. A communications link connects IST to Cybershare's Control Data system, while providing Cybershare access to IST's IBM equipment.

"IST has really cut a niche for themselves in Quebec as the only Quebec-based and Quebec-owned company of its kind," a member of the industry comments. "Although they have a national charter, their big success continues to be in Quebec."

In the West, Bill Tennant and Norman Song formed Tennant, Song and Associates to provide customized computer applications and turnkey systems. The Vancouver company, which began operations in 1971, was acquired three years later by Boeing Computer Services, a U.S. firm (and a division of the Boeing Aircraft organization) with a computer complex in Seattle, Washington. Boeing Computer Services Canada Ltd., with Norman Song as president, has branches in Calgary and Edmonton.

At the time that Winnipeg-based Symbionics went bankrupt, R. Angus Ltd. of Edmonton, a distributor of heavy construction equipment, was interested in diversifying its business activities. In April, 1971, R. Angus purchased the Edmonton operation of Datamation Centres which had merged with Symbionics in 1970.

The company formed a new corporation, R. Angus Computer Services. Toward the end of the seventies, because of an expanding base of external business, R. Angus Alberta Ltd. decided to divest itself of its computer business. In 1979, R. Angus Computer Services entered an affiliation with Advanced Computer Techniques Corporation of New York, a software consulting firm owned by Charles P. Lecht. The Canadian operation's name was changed at that time to ACT Computer Services Ltd.

On Canada's eastern coast, the largest indigenous service bureau in the Maritimes is Maritime Computer Limited, incorporated in 1976. Maritime Computer is a subsidiary of Maritime Telephone and Telegraph, which became involved with the services business when it acquired Consolidated Computer's Halifax branch.

However, probably the most significant concentration of computer technology in Atlantic Canada is the University of New Brunswick in Fredericton. With an IBM 3032 processor, the university provides services to Maritime universities, government organizations, and certain private businesses.

Looking after provincial government needs

Across Canada during the seventies, government owned and operated service companies began to provide data processing facilities for provincial government departments and agencies.

In the Maritimes, the Nova Scotia provincial government's bureau of computer/communications is BMCS (Bureau of Management Consulting and Computer/Communications Services). BMCS acts as a centralized agency, providing processing and systems services for government departments and acting as the vehicle through which contracts are let out to the private sector.

In the province of Quebec, a central bureau to meet the data processing needs of government departments was created in 1976. The bureau Central de l'Informatique (BCI) was charged with co-ordinating inter-department information processing and providing data processing services to government departments and organizations. Its mandate included the development of policies on government acquisition of data processing goods and services from the private sector.

Heading the bureau from its inception until 1979 was Gaston Beauséjour, assistant deputy minister, Quebec Department of Communications. M. Beauséjour had begun his career as a systems engineer and manager with IBM Canada. Later, as has been noted, he was a consultant and vice president with Aquila-BST, and afterwards was associated first with the Quebec and then with the federal government. In 1982, he joined DMR et Associés.

In the west, SaskComp (the Saskatchewan Computer Utility Corporation) and Manitoba Data Services are operated by their respective provincial governments. SaskComp was created in 1973 to provide computer services to government and other Crown corporations in Saskatchewan. With computing facilities based in Regina and Saskatoon, SaskComp supports remote batch and interactive terminals throughout the province.

Manitoba Data Services was formed in 1976. Services provided to provincial government departments include customized application development, data preparation, timesharing, and remote job entry.

However, the largest of the provincial government computer service companies is British Columbia Systems Corporation (BCSC). BCSC was created by the provincial legislature as a Crown corporation in 1977. Its mandate was to provide all data processing services required by provincial government ministries and by other designated government organizations. BCSC was also given the authority to serve certain public sector organizations including municipalities, hospitals, school districts, and universities.

Victoria-based BCSC officially began operation as a Crown corporation in April 1978. D.A. (Don) Alexander, formerly an assistant deputy minister in Ontario's Ministry of Government Services, was appointed president and chief executive officer.

In the first two years of operation, the corporation's workload doubled. After three years, with 1980–1981 revenues of more than $49 million, BCSC had become a leading Canadian data services organization.

"The first responsibility for a public sector service bureau is to improve problem solving capabilities and systems within the government itself," Mr. Alexander says. "The second part of their role is to enhance the private sector data processing industry through government purchasing power and by acting as a catalyst for activities in the private sector."

Where appropriate, BCSC contracts with private data service organizations for the provision of services for the corporation's clients. In 1976, before the incorporation of BCSC, the province let out about $100,000 worth of data processing services work. In 1980–81, services worth almost $10.4 million were let out to private companies, with more than 96 per cent of this work contracted to firms in British Columbia.

Software, systems houses and success

As has been previously mentioned, software for various makes and models of computer equipment had become big business by the mid-seventies.

Systemhouse Ltd. of Ottawa has a history going back to 1968 when Jack Davies had started a company called Softwarehouse Ltd. after leaving the vice presidency of Welby Computer Services. The company was acquired in 1971 by Systems Dimensions Ltd. and Mr. Davies became a vice president of SDL. He saw that there was a demand for applications capability that was not really being represented on the marketplace and broke away again to form Systemhouse Ltd. in 1974 along with John Kelly.

By the beginning of the 1980s, the company had branches in every major city across Canada and had also branched out into the lucrative U.S. market with an office in Washington. Jack Davies had also decided to change the direction of the company from consulting into software development.

Systemhouse went public in June 1980 and was listed on the Toronto Stock Exchange in November 1980. The company had been growing at about 70 per cent annually and had to look to equity financing to support the product development. Since going public, Systemhouse has attracted a great deal of attention with well-publicized announcements of losses during its 1982 fiscal year.

Another Ottawa-based software house, Quasar Systems Ltd., has demonstrated phenomenal growth since it was formed in 1969 by Michael Potter. Quasar has expanded from a two-man operation in the early seventies to a company employing more than 200 people in the early eighties. The company started as a consulting and professional services firm, but changed its perspective with the beginning of the eighties. It now provides software for a range of Hewlett-Packard computer equipment.

Quasar sells its software products world wide, with some 80 per cent of product sales occurring in the United States. Michael

Potter expects to take his company public some time before the middle of the eighties.

The software/system house business has not been a bed of roses for the many companies in this market sector. There have been some well-publicized failures in Canada over the years. Two of these have been Systems Approach Limited and Art Benjamin Associates.

Systems Approach Limited was started as a consulting and computer products firm by Terrance Ortt in 1973. That year, the firm had revenues of $100,000 with promise of a rosy future. SAL had taken on the distribution of the Computer Automation IM/70 remote job entry terminal and was providing an SAL-developed graphics language called Grapple that was well-regarded by the architectural and engineering professions. By 1977, Systems Approach had revenues of about $3 million.

However, the bubble burst at the end of 1979, and Systems Approach closed its doors. The consulting side of the business was sold to Hickling-Smith Limited. Control Data Canada bought the sales and services operations, and a group of former SAL employees set up a company called Phoenix Graphics Ltd. to carry on the work that had been started in interactive graphics with Grapple.

Art Benjamin and Joseph Pilarski left IBM in January 1977 to launch a consulting and education firm called Art Benjamin Associates (ABA). Perhaps the company is best known for the development of a software product called Act/1, a package that was designed to increase the productivity of computer software developers by helping them to create other software.

Act/1 had been well received by users in Canada and the United States and ABA had worked out a financing agreement with the Federal Enterprise Development Board, through the Ministry of Industry, Trade and Commerce. In early 1982, the financing from ITC was cancelled. The company closed its doors in March 1982 because there was no financing to continue the development of its Act/2 software package.

However, Art Benjamin soon started another company called Online People Inc. to do consulting and education—"but no software," according to Mr. Benjamin. And the Act/1 software product received a reprieve. Bailey & Rose Ltd. of Toronto, a data processing consulting firm with offices in Toronto, Ottawa, Montreal, Halifax, Vancouver, Edmonton, and San Francisco, contracted to continue the maintenance and development of Act/1.

The more we get together...

The *ad hoc* group of service companies that had joined forces in 1969 to protest CN/CP Telecommunications' purchase of an interest in Computer Sciences Canada was the first step toward the formation of an organization oriented toward promoting the interests of computer services companies.

The Canadian Association of Data Processing Service Organizations (CADAPSO) was formed in 1970 by a group of Canadian computing service firms as a forum for expressing ideas about the industry and a means of liaison with government agencies. The association's purpose is to "promote, foster, and maintain the computer service industry in Canada."

Originally, the association functioned as a chapter of the U.S. ADAPSO (Association of Data Processing Service Organizations). ADAPSO had been formed in 1960 by a group that included Clifford Green, then president of the Toronto-based Statistical Reporting and Tabulating Ltd. Mr. Green was not only a charter member of ADAPSO, but also served as president of the U.S. organization from 1962 to 1963.

In 1972, the Canadian chapter decided it should be an independent organization in order to deal more effectively with the fast-growing Canadian services industry. CADAPSO was officially incorporated in 1973, but maintains a group membership in ADAPSO.

A roll call of its presidents indicates the caliber of the organization. The first president was Malcolm Welch, president of Welby Computing Services. He was followed by Don McPhail, president of Comtech International, Joseph Paradi, Dataline president, and Norman Williams of Systems Dimensions Limited. Subsequent presidents were Richard Taylor, William Boggs, and Gerry Meinzer, presidents of Datacrown, Canada Systems Group, and Real Time Datapro respectively. Derek Price of Comshare became the first two-year president, and later Gerry Meinzer and Joseph

Paradi each accepted the presidency for a second term.

CADAPSO protects members' interests by promoting the industry, offering unique industry-related services, and providing accurate information for use in government decision-making. It maintains committees on banking, telecommunications, software, transborder data flow, and government relations. The organization also collects and publishes industry statistics. With regional chapters in Quebec, Ontario, and Western Canada, CADAPSO has grown from a membership of 24 companies in 1973 to more than 70 in 1982.

"In the beginning, CADAPSO's major interest was to enlighten the government about the industry," says Dr. Paradi, 1981–82 president. "Today, our major interest is in providing member services and strengthening the industry as a strong and vibrant part of the Canadian scene."

Both CADAPSO and ADAPSO have been active participants in organizing and taking part in world computing conferences that have been held in Barcelona (1978), San Francisco (1980), and Copenhagen (1982). In 1986, the world conference is scheduled for Toronto.

A rift within the CADAPSO organization developed over the issue of whether chartered banks should be able to provide data processing, particularly payroll, services.

William Loewen, whose company Comcheq Services Ltd. of Winnipeg is the largest payroll data processing firm in Canada, felt that his views were not being adequately represented within the CADAPSO structure. There were other small computing services firms that felt likewise.

In late 1980, this group of small service firms formed the Canadian Independent Computer Services Association (CICSA) and broke away from CADAPSO.

In 1982 president of CICSA is Ronald Ross, president of Central Computing Services Ltd. of Winnipeg, a firm that specializes in accounting services.

Another association worthy of mention is CATA (the Canadian Advanced Technology Association) formed in 1977. "CATA is significant not just as an association *per se*, but as an indication that by 1977 there were enough active Canadian high technology companies to warrant an association," comments industry consultant Bill Hutchison. "And it's interesting that the founding meeting took place at the same time that the International Federation for Information Processing (IFIP) conference was first held in Canada."

In addition to Mr. Hutchison, the early organizers of CATA were Mike Cowpland of Mitel, Des Cunningham of Gandalf, Gordon Hutchison, publisher of *The Electronics Communicator*, an industry newsletter, Mark Norton of Norpak, and Terrance Ortt of Systems Approach Limited.

The organization's membership has grown to about 100 companies, many of which have had yearly growth rates of 50 to 100 per cent. Average annual growth has been 20 per cent. In 1980, revenues generated by CATA firms (excluding Northern Telecom) were $300 million.

In retrospect

During the seventies there were more users than ever before and they were increasingly sophisticated in the application of computers to meet their business problems, according to Honeywell's Pat Suddick. "That changed the complexion of the business," he says.

"And the generation that's now coming up—using calculators, playing computer games, etc.—the computer is not a mystery, but simply another tool."

Epilog

THE FUTURE OF the Canadian data processing industry holds great promise—particularly in software expertise, data communications equipment, and know-how.

However, the industry has not proved to be completely immune to the pinch of the 1981–82 economic climate. The industry was once thought to be recession proof, with growth rates of about 20 to 30 per cent annually over all sectors. The economic uncertainty of the eighties has affected the large multinationals, computing services firms, software houses, small manufacturers, and the user community. Lean times have meant belt tightening and revised game plans throughout the industry.

This fact is reflected in the stock market reports of 1982. Some of the high technology stocks, such as Mitel Corp. and Lumonics, continued to do well. Others, such as Systemhouse and Cableshare fell drastically, their results causing a general downturn in high tech industrials. However, in spite of the poor economic climate, new listings in this area continued to appear.

Issues such as transborder data flow, privacy and security, government regulation or deregulation, and government involvement in the computer industry continued to cause debate in the eighties. These conflicts may take time to be resolved. But while they are being debated, the day to day operations of users and suppliers are being affected.

Aside from oil, natural gas, forests, fish, grain, water, and hydro-electric power, perhaps Canada's newest and most effective natural resource is its people—those in particular who are involved in the data processing industry. Many are worried that, if a great deal of care is not exercised, the computer industry may suffer the fate of the Canadian aircraft and automobile industries, whose failures have been attributed to a Canadian "inferiority complex."

It is interesting to read reports coming out of the United States saying that, in reality, the Canadians consider themselves to be superior to their neighbors to the south.

By the 1980s, the heady beginning years of data processing in Canada were behind. Ahead were new and difficult challenges to be met in the dawning information age. There were better machines to be built, more effective software to be created, more productive applications to be developed.

The potential appears to be limited only by the bounds of human imagination, and the ability of people to make things happen.

Index